EXPLORING ENVIRONMENTAL CAREERS

by

Stanley Jay Shapiro

THE ROSEN PUBLISHING GROUP, INC.

NEW YORK

To Rachel and Marjorie,
whom I love very much

Also by Stanley Jay Shapiro
Exploring Careers in Science

Published in 1982, 1985 by
The Rosen Publishing Group, Inc.
29 East 21st Street, New York City, New York 10010

Revised Edition, 1985
Copyright 1982, 1985, by Stanley Jay Shapiro

Library of Congress Cataloging in Publication Data

Shapiro, Stanley Jay.
  Exploring environmental careers.

  (Exploring careers)
  1. Environmental protection—Vocational guidance.
I. Title. II. Series: Exploring careers (New York,
N.Y.)
TD170.2.S45   363.7'0023   82-5216
ISBN 0-8239-0555-1   AACR2

Manufactured in the United States of America.

About the Author

Stanley Shapiro is a teacher of chemistry at James Madison High School in Brooklyn, New York. He specializes in working with gifted teenagers who want to pursue professional careers in science, mathematics, and medicine.

Dr. Shapiro grew up in Washington, D.C., where, through the public school science fair program, he developed an interest in science. As a high school student, he won more than twenty local and national awards, including three National First Place Awards in the Future Scientists of America Science Fair, the Academy of Science Medal, the Dow Chemical Award, the Smithsonian Award, and the Honors Group Award of the Westinghouse Science Talent Search.

He received a bachelor of science degree in chemistry from the American University in Washington, D.C., and a master's degree in organic chemistry from New York University. Dr. Shapiro received a doctorate in science education from New York University in 1978. His research study was *A Multimedia Project for the Independent Instruction of Allied Health Students in the Application of Mathematical Skills to Science Problems in Their Curricula.*

From 1974 to 1977 he was the science curriculum specialist for the Division of Allied Health at New York City Community College, City University of New York. At the college, he worked on the development of a multimedia learning center, where students could use television, audiotapes, slides, filmstrips, workbooks, and laboratory facilities to learn science skills. Prior to that he was a biochemist for the Gillette Research Institute, an assistant conservator for the Smithsonian Institution, and a science writer for the NBC-TV show *It's Academic.*

Dr. Shapiro is a member of the American Association for the Advancement of Science, the National Science Teachers Association, Phi Delta Kappa, the American Chemical Society, the Chemistry Teachers Club, the New York Zoological Society, and the Science Council of New York City. He is a consultant to the National Science Foundation on teacher development projects in science.

He lives in New York City with his wife, Marjorie, his daughter, Rachel, and two cats. He enjoys golf, swimming, theatre, ballet, and chamber music.

Acknowledgments

The information gathered for this book came from many sources. The most important were the *Environmental Protection Careers Guidebook,* the *Occupational Outlook Handbook, 1980-81 Edition, Exploring Careers,* and the *Guide for Occupational Exploration* by the U.S. Department of Labor's Bureau of Labor Statistics. The U.S. Department of Energy provided information regarding energy careers throughout the 1980's. *Environmental Quality,* a report to the Congress of the United States by the Council on Environmental Quality, provided valuable details on the state of the global environment.

I wish to thank the following private corporations for their generous help and the photographs showing people working to aid both mankind and the environment: Phillips Petroleum Company, Exxon Corporation, 3M Corporation, and Consolidated Edison.

Preface to the Second Edition

New administrations, new concerns, and new problems regarding the protection of our environment have necessitated updating of this book. There have been substantial increases in the starting salaries of scientists and engineers; regrettably, however, there are few new jobs for oceanographers, meteorologists, or nuclear plant workers.

This new edition has an entirely new section, Chapter IX, which discusses the nontechnical, nonscientific occupations dealing with the protection of the environment. Those include the legal and political career opportunities involving environmental protection, as well as professional jobs in occupational health and regional planning. You will learn about the interrelated roles of the Environmental Protection Agency, the Occupational Safety and Health Administration, and the citizen groups that try to work in concert to safeguard the public, the workplace, and the delicate ecosystem.

Contents

v

Introduction

Among the nine planets that orbit our sun, only on earth does life flourish. On earth there is a complex relationship of forces that we call nature. Nature allows the rain to fall continuously in a cycle of precipitation—cultivation—evaporation. Flowers bloom and produce seeds for future blossoms. Fish feed on small microbic plankton and become themselves food for larger species. Prairies elevate and mountains erode to flatlands. In nature's design bees turn pollen to honey, lionesses hunt for their pride, birds migrate over thousands of miles, and human babies rise up from their crawl to take their first upright steps.

In earth's cosmic passage from gaseous condensate to its multifarious life forms, mankind may be only a small detail. Without man, nature would continue to regenerate according to its laws of physics, chemistry, and evolution. With man, the delicate balance has been perilously shifted, and only man can set it right again.

The earth provides resources that feed, clothe, and provide shelter for us. But in recent times we have been draining its riches for opulent living, entertainment and recreation, communication and transportation, decoration, industrialization, and all of the other comforts of our modern civilized society. It has now become evident that the use of nature must be carefully controlled.

In this book, we shall explore how we can use and develop our planet sensibly, leaving it as unharmed and as undamaged as possible so that tomorrow's generations can also thrive. We shall look at how the environment works, and how people can work with nature. This is a book about careers that serve the requirements of man as well as the needs of nature.

Chapter **1**

The Environment

In this chapter we shall discuss the basic terminology, factors, and problems involved in dealing with the environment. There are four sections in this chapter. The first, "What Is the Environment?", provides the definitions and concepts needed for understanding how nature's delicate balance is maintained. The second section, "Mankind's Impact on the Environment," tells how the advance of civilization brought about, usually unknowingly, the environment's deterioration. The third part, "The Condition of the Earth's Resources Today," explores the effects of industrialization, overpopulation, and uncontrolled development on the limited supplies available. The last section, "How We Can Use the Earth and Still Protect the Environment," tells about the conservation movement and how concerned citizens and politicians work together with planners, scientists, engineers, developers, industry, energy companies, craftsmen, educators, and writers in an effort to continue the growth of our country without endangering nature.

A. WHAT IS THE ENVIRONMENT?

Think for a moment about where you live. What do you see surrounding you? Take a sheet of paper and list the objects that are within 100 yards of your chair.

Did you remember the air? How many living things are on your list? What objects could be eliminated and not change your life at all? Should light and heat be on your list? What about water? If you live in a large city, how would your list differ from that of someone who lived on a farm? Would your survival needs differ? Would these needs be met in the same way?

The *environment* is your surroundings. It is the aggregate (collection) of things, conditions, and influences around you. The total environment can be divided into the *physical environment*, which consists of things that are not alive, and the *biological environment*, which is made up of only living things.

3

Land, water, and air are the three primary constituents of the physical environment. They may, of course, be considered separately, or their influences may be combined, as in the phenomenon of weather.

The physical environment is not only composed of matter; there is also a nonmolecular aspect to it. Temperature and the amount of sunlight are important energy factors that do not have weight or take up space. When considering the environment, it is important to be able to think beyond the simple and the obvious. Earth's environment is a complex, ever-changing condition.

In the *biological environment* are *producers, consumers,* and *decomposers.* The producers are the green plants, which have the unique ability to make their own food. The consumers are the animals who must depend on other living things, both plant and animal, for their food. The decomposers break down or decay the waste products of animals and the bodies of dead plants and animals. All three groups combine in a complicated scheme called the *food chain,* or better, *food web.*

Throughout the biological environment are situations that influence the health and growth of organisms (living things). These factors can be physical, such as the type of soil present and the nutrients it holds or the amount of rainfall, or the factors can be biological, such as the absence or presence of prey or predators. There can also be social factors, such as crowding. And there can be events that are relatively new, such as air and water pollution, noise, nuclear waste, land development, strip mining, and so on.

The environment is a living system, forever changing and forever adapting. Often the term *ecosystem* is used in discussing the relationships between the multiple environmental factors. An ecosystem is an interacting unit made up of the living community and its nonliving environment. An ecosystem might be a pond, a stream, a forest, a meadow, a desert, a seaside village, an arctic tundra, or a metropolis. An aquarium with a stable, unchanging, living community is an artificial ecosystem. Millions of ecosystems exist on the earth.

Ecosystems, too, evolve. The parts played by separate biologic species or by unique physical factors may become more important or may disappear completely. Nature is continually modifying our world. Nature's method of biologic change is called natural selection and requires thousands of centuries for adaptations to occur. Civilization has usurped nature's gradual process. The environment is tough. It can usually bounce back from terrible shocks and traumas, but it is vital that it not be struck a mortal blow that will destroy it.

As we discuss the role of man and his influence on the environment, there are two important principles to keep in mind:

1. *Everything in the environment is related to everything else.*
2. *The environment is very complex, but this complexity is, in part, responsible for its stability.*

Mankind tends to reduce complexity. A forest contains many cross-connected food and propagation (reproduction) links, as well as numerous soil–weather–light variations. These all contribute to the adaptability and stability of the woods. However, when man plants a field with only one crop, such as wheat, this reduces the complexity of the ecosystem. The wheat field is highly vulnerable to changes in water supply, insects, weeds, birds, rodents, and disease. A quick change can easily mean the destruction of the crop. A forest, because of its complexity, is not nearly so vulnerable and can adapt to many changes.

Man's attempt to simplify for the short run forces him to use chemical insecticides and herbicides. These unnatural intrusions into the ecosystem can cause imbalances that may poison the soil or contaminate the water supply, which may eventually cause hardship and expense.

B. MANKIND'S IMPACT ON THE ENVIRONMENT

For fifty thousand years people have been modifying the environment to improve their lives. Neolithic (Stone Age) man used fire to substantially change his ecosystem. Hunters would set fire to a savannah to herd mammoths over a cliff. Early farmers would burn down a forest, so that crops could be planted. Infestation would be eliminated by a scorching blaze.

When man began to settle in villages, about ten thousand years ago, he had to clear the land so that he could raise domesticated plants and animals. Occasionally he burned down too much forest. Sometimes his goats overgrazed too much rangeland. And often his agriculture techniques depleted the soil and eroded the land. When these events happened, the environment became barren, and the settler was forced to move on. Some scientists believe that such factors may have caused the well-watered grasslands of northern Africa to change into the vast deserts that exist there today. *Desertification,* the turning of land into desert, is still causing thousands of acres of arable (capable of producing crops) land to become wasted each year. There are villages where people are watching the desert take over their fields, just as seaside towns watch the ocean nibbling away the coastline.

As civilization developed, its relationship with nature became more involved. Religions were invented to help people understand and deal with the various phenomena that affected their lives. Mythological gods and totems protected tribes and towns, while demons wreaked havoc and devastation. The "modern" religions evolved from the early, mystical supernatural beings that governed the tides, the crops, fertility, fire, the sun, and so on.

Curiously, there is a significant difference between the religions of the West (Judaism, Christianity, and Islam) and those that developed in the East (Hinduism, Buddhism, Confucianism, Taoism). The Western religions stress a single god, whereas the Eastern religions are not concerned with that notion. Hinduism has a multitude of gods, and followers of Buddhism, Confucianism, and Taoism do not necessarily believe in a god at all.

The Eastern and Western religions also have far different attitudes toward man's relationship with nature. Eastern religions, for the past three thousand years, tended to stress the idea that man should live in harmony with nature. Western ideologies held the opposite view. The Judeo–Christian–Muslim attitude has been to subdue and use the earth. "Be fruitful and multiply...Have dominion over the fish of the sea and over the birds of the air and over every living thing that moves upon the earth."

Western man set about to conquer nature. The *scientific method* of drawing conclusions based only on careful observation of the real world began to develop about eight hundred years ago in Europe. The scientific study of nature resulted in a technology that increased productivity and led to the agricultural and industrial revolutions. Individual farmers became more productive, and it became possible for them to support a larger percentage of the population off the farm. This off-farm population was then free to work in the factories, and cities began to grow. Manufactured goods replaced the work of craftsmen. Bankers, clerks, lawyers, and tradespeople were needed to provide services for the workers and the manufacturers. And ever-increasing sources of energy were required to fuel mankind's progress.

There were also problems associated with this spectacular rise. The inequity of low wages and rising costs coupled with inhumane working conditions produced labor strife. The burning of wood seriously depleted the forests of Europe until coal became popular in the early eighteenth century. But the coal, which was in heavy demand following the invention of the steam engine in 1765, was provided by miners who worked in hazardous, unhealthful conditions, and the soot and wastes ejected from the smokestacks blackened the air of the cities.

Today, the wonders of the modern world have to be weighed against the ill effects of air pollution, highways, insecticides, radiation, ghetto life, crime, and all the rest. Still, our life is so much improved by the miracles of science and technology that it would seem ridiculous to lament their invention despite our hindsighted knowledge of the environmental problems they produced. In fact, one of the worst offenders, the automobile, was initially heralded as a boon, a benefit, to a clean-air society since it could eliminate that dreadful polluter, the horse.

Our lives are filled and enriched by the products and services developed by the entrepreneurs, which have, in many places, befouled and denigrated the land and its people. Some, probably, were motivated by greed and were aware of the consequences that would develop, but many corporations had little knowledge of the ill effects that would ensue.

An example of how good intentions turned ill is the story of DDT. The chemical DDT (short for dichloro-diphenyl-trichloro-ethane) was first synthesized by a German chemist in 1874, but its properties as an *insecticide* (killer of insects) were not discovered until 1939. Immediately DDT was hailed as a means of stamping out insect-borne disease and winning the farmers' war against crop destroyers overnight. Nonfarmers, too, would naturally benefit from this remarkable discovery, since the prices a household pays for farm products are based on the quantity and quality of the harvest. If insect destruction could be eliminated, the cost of agricultural products would come down.

The use of DDT marked the beginning of the "green revolution" in the underdeveloped countries of Asia and Africa. For hundreds of generations, locusts, grasshoppers, and other insect pests have ravaged their fields. With one fly-over by a crop duster, the dreams of millions of poor farmers could be realized. Bountiful harvests appeared on lands that were usually scarred and mutilated by pests.

Thus DDT was hailed by the scientists and political leaders of the world. Its discoverer, Paul Müller of Switzerland, was awarded the Nobel Prize. Its use was prescribed, in most cases, with the best interests of mankind and nature in mind. Only later was it found to be, in the words of Rachel Carson, the "elixir of death."

The chemical was found to be lethal to birds, small animals, fish, and man. The spraying of forests in Wisconsin to prevent Dutch elm disease eliminated robins, hawks, owls, chickadees, nuthatches, titmice, woodpeckers, and, to some extent, raccoons, opossums, shrews, and moles. When chickens ate grain from plants sprayed with the insecticide, the shells of their eggs were too thin, and no chicks were born. Following a crop dusting in Flint Creek, Alabama, 94 percent of the bass, sunfish, carp, shad, and catfish in the area were killed. DDT has been found to attack the human brain and blood, to affect the manufacture of genetic material, and to be a *carcinogen* (a producer of cancer).

There are other examples that illustrate how "improvements" for our standard of living caused environmental problems. Phosphates were put in laundry detergents because consumers liked "cleaner, brighter" wash, but this additive seriously contaminated streams and groundwater in certain communities. Power companies are encouraged to produce cheaper and greater amounts of electricity for industry and housing developers, but coal- and oil-burning plants produce air pollution and force dependence on fuel resources (which may be foreign), and nuclear power has its own peculiar side effects. The synthetic textile industry (which makes nylon, orlon, rayon, and other polyester materials) and the plastics manufacturers both need oil, which once consumed is not replenished by nature.

Coal is mentioned as a necessary replacement for oil, since the United States' coal reserves can last for a few hundred more years before they, too, are depleted. But the inexpensive mining of coal often requires the stripping of square miles of natural terrain. Methods of mining beneath the surface are dangerous and much more expensive, and the extra costs would have to be paid by the consumer.

In Crested Butte, Colorado, a mountain is filled with molybdenum. Molybdenum is a strategic metal used to strengthen steel and to make fertilizer, rubber, lubricants, plastics, and paint. In the past, the discovery of a billion-dollar resource would have been joyously celebrated by the townspeople. The hopes of a boom town generating lots of revenue would have been very exciting. Today, however, the village is fighting the development of the molybdenum mountain, because the residents fear that their quiet, rustic life would be seriously altered and that the area's ecosystem might be disturbed. This is a preservation-versus-progress fight that is, perhaps, as disruptive as the range wars that bloodily pitted the cattlemen, sheep herders, and farmers against each other at the end of the nineteenth century.

Environmental problems are not simple, and their solutions cannot be straightforward. Society needs, even demands, progress, but we still must protect the earth for ourselves and for nature's countless species. It is necessary to use the riches of the earth, but not in a manner that will destroy it. It is possible to do this, and the technologies that will have to be invented will require well-trained, open-minded, talented people. Future environmental careers must involve people who not only know how to improve our lives, but who can also preserve the resources of nature.

C. THE CONDITION OF THE EARTH'S RESOURCES TODAY

If present trends continue, the world in 2000 will be more crowded, more polluted, less stable ecologically, and more vulnerable to disruption than the world we live in now. Serious stress involving population, resources, and environment are clearly visible ahead. Despite greater material output, the world's people will be poorer in many ways than they are today.

For hundreds of millions of the desperately poor, the outlook for food and other necessities of life will be no better. For many it will be worse. Barring revolutionary advances in technology, life for most people on earth will be more precarious in 2000 than it is now — unless the nations of the world act decisively to alter current trends.[1]

As we begin the 1980's there are signs of a degraded world environment. Many living resources, both plant and animal, are being destroyed or depleted. It appears as if the planet's capacity to support people is being irreversibly reduced in both developed and developing countries.

The rapid growth in world population is putting a greater stress on the limited resources available. In 1980 there was an increase of about 75 million people over the population in 1979. It is predicted that in the year 2000 the annual growth rate of world population will be 100 million people each year. More than 90 percent of this rise will take place in poorer, less developed countries.

The supply of fresh water, timber, and marine fish, all of which are essential human resources, will decline, causing prices to rise. The growing stock of wood per capita (for each person) is expected to drop almost in half. The per capita water supply will decline by almost one-third, simply because more people will be consuming the same amount of fresh water. And the harvesting of marine fish will probably not increase over the next twenty years.

The capacity of the earth to provide enough food for all was examined in detail by the Presidential Commission on World Hunger. The report noted that a crisis of global food supply even more serious than the current energy crisis could occur within twenty years, and that it is likely unless steps are taken now to increase food production significantly in the developing nations.

A serious threat to the biological environment is the rapid disappearance of tropical forests. Extensive cutting of tropical forests is causing loss of agricultural soils, siltation (the choking of streams by fine sand and sediment), and intensified flooding. If present trends continue, tropical deforestation could be responsible for the extinction of as much as 10 percent of the world's plant and animal species in the next two decades. Further, extensive loss of forests might aggravate the rising concentrations of carbon dioxide in the earth's atmosphere.

---

[1] Council on Environmental Quality and U.S. Department of State, *The Global 2000 Report to the President: Entering the Twenty-First Century,* Vol. One, Washington, DC: U.S. Government Printing Office, 1980, p. 1.

There is a growing realization that the earth's atmosphere could be permanently and disastrously altered by human actions. The burning of fossil fuels, such as coal, oil, and natural gas, is causing a steady, measurable buildup of carbon dioxide in the atmosphere that threatens widespread climate change. The burning also leads to the formation of acids in the atmosphere that may fall in rain or snow hundreds of miles from their source. The effects of acid rain are not fully understood, but it may be seriously damaging forests, crops, and soil.

The National Academy of Sciences has confirmed reports that the continued use of freon and other chlorofluorocarbons in aerosol spray cans will significantly decrease the earth's protective layer of ozone. As ozone concentrations decrease, the intensity of biologically damaging ultraviolet radiation (the light energy that causes sunburn, and worse) in natural daylight increases. Continued use of these chemicals could eventually cause several hundred thousand more cases of skin cancer per year in the United States.

There seems to be a natural tendency to regard the oceans as a convenient, limitless receptacle for waste. Experience and understanding are teaching us that, despite their vastness, the oceans' natural ability to receive, decompose, and recycle wastes has limits. But as problems of waste disposal on land multiply, pressures to use the oceans as a dumping ground become stronger.

If present trends continue, the result will be worsening poverty and human suffering, resource waste, environmental destruction, and a rising potential for international strife. But this is based on the assumption that public policies will remain unchanged. It is hoped that governments and corporations will change.

D. HOW WE CAN USE THE EARTH AND STILL PROTECT THE ENVIRONMENT

The census of 1890 disclosed that the American frontier was effectively closed. Before then, Americans held the notion that the natural resources of this country were inexhaustible. Some resources, like the forests, were even considered an obstruction to development. The Homestead Act of 1862 gave title to Federal land to any person who settled and worked the property for five years. It was presumed that if the land was forested, you had to clear it before it could be farmed. Our natural resources were considered limitless.

At the turn of the century, however, when Theodore Roosevelt was President, it became clear that unlimited exploitation of our natural resources, especially our forests, was not to be desired. The professional forester Gifford Pinchot wrote in 1907, "The idea was that all these natural resources which we had been dealing with as though they were in watertight compartments actually constituted one united problem. That problem was the use of the earth for the permanent good of man....The idea was so new that it did not even have a name....Finally Overton Price suggested that we should call it 'conservation' and the President [Roosevelt] said 'O.K.' So we called it the conservation movement."

Within the conservation movement, however, there are varying concepts and policies. Some define it as a means for more properly or more equitably developing our natural resources, such as reseeding and cultivating timberland to replace trees needed for housing, rayon, paper, and furniture. Although the forests are beautiful and are the refuge for wilderness creatures, many believe that these factors are secondary to the commercial use of the timber.

Another group of conservationists feel that we should preserve wild things for their own sake. The naturalist John Muir felt great reverence for the Sierra Nevada. "Benevolent, solemn, fateful, pervaded with divine light, every landscape glows like a countenance hallowed in eternal repose; and every one of its living creatures, clad in flesh and leaves, and every crystal of its rocks, whether on the surface shining in the sun or buried miles deep in what we call darkness, is throbbing and pulsing with the heartbeats of God." This viewpoint calls for the halting of a hundred million dollar hydroelectric dam to save a school of snail darters whose existence would be imperiled by the project, or the barring of oil exploration on wilderness acreage controlled by the Federal government.

Clearly the problems of the protection and the use of nature are many and complex. No simple set of policies will guarantee the continued survival and improvement of mankind. In this book, then, we shall discuss careers in which both concerns can be arbitrated. There are jobs that develop and use nature, and there are those that oversee the use so that as little harm as possible occurs. Both branches work together in order that we can maintain and improve our way of living without damaging our planet.

The effective use of nature requires careful planning by the Federal government, states, regions, cities, towns, and neighborhoods. Urban planners, regional commissions, and environmental consultants have staffs that look into the environmental and economic variables before any project is started. Good planning can foresee problems before they occur. Careers in planning involve knowledge and often expertise in diverse areas such as pollution, transportation, employment, water supply, education, health, and fire and police protection.

To follow carefully considered plans, architects and designers are needed who will compose the ideas onto blueprints and models. Engineers are needed to carry out these projects, applying the theories and principles of science and mathematics to practical technical problems.

The engineers rely on scientists, mathematicians, and other researchers for information about the land, the watershed, the weather, and the new technologies and products available. The scientists try to discover less polluting, quieter, stronger, sturdier, lighter, longer-lasting, less expensive materials and methods.

Many scientists and engineers work for industrialists who develop and manufacture goods and who contract out the services needed for production. These industrialists, along with bankers and economists, provide the economic structure through which raw materials and imaginative concepts are processed into our modern way of life.

Politicians, legislators, and government employees work along with private benevolent organizations to oversee and protect the environment. There are special regulations and laws on standards for clean air, safe drinking water, toxic substances, radiation, and noise. There are statutes for protecting the worker and the environment.

The communications industry uses newspapers, radio, television, and magazines to keep us informed on environmental problems and how people are going about solving them, or, in some instances, causing them.

Educators are a special resource. They teach their students the values of environmental control and the hazards that can occur if care is not taken.

All of these fields are involved in protecting the environment. Within these areas many occupations exist. Some require advanced skills and special abilities. Others are open to anyone who wants to work hard and has a special interest in a career that can benefit mankind and the planet.

Managing the Global Environment

This chapter describes the five main categories in which people are working in the environment. The first category involves protecting and safeguarding the environment. The main areas of concern in environmental protection are water quality, air quality, toxic substance control, noise control, and solid waste management.

The second category discusses the relationship between living things and the environment — ecology. The proper management of the nation's land is the major concern that is discussed in the third section of this chapter. The fourth deals with the production of energy, which is vital to our country's maintenance and growth.

The last section discusses the role of the environmental sciences in basic and applied fields. It briefly explains how geologists, geophysicists, meteorologists, and oceanographers are helping us understand our planet, and how they are trying to find methods for solving the problems that are damaging our resources.

A. ENVIRONMENTAL PROTECTION

1. Water Quality

Wastewater comes from industry, agriculture, and humans. Municipal sewage is over 99 percent water. It contains the liquid wastes from homes, schools, hotels, and hospitals. It contains bacteria, viruses, and hazardous chemicals. Public sewer systems dump 40 billion gallons of waste daily.

Thousands of industrial plants discharge billions of gallons of waste into our waterways each day. Much of it is inadequately treated; some is not treated at all. *Effluents* (anything that flows) from a paper mill may contain cellulose on which bacteria can thrive. This waste can easily putrefy a stream. A processing plant may release sulfuric acid into a harbor that will subsequently cause serious damage.

A huge volume of storm water drains into waterways every day, bringing with it tons of pollutants and eroded soil. More than 62 million tons of garbage, sludge, chemicals, explosives, debris, and dirt are dumped into our waters annually. In addition, about 8,500 accidental and deliberate oil spills contaminate coastal and inland waters each year.

Agriculture contributes its share of pollutants. Animal waste in the Potomac River basin is almost six times that of human waste. Agricultural insecticides, fungicides, and herbicides may increase crop yields, but they are also washed into our water systems.

Water need not be dirty to be polluted. Power plants and many industries borrow some 130 billion gallons of water each day for cooling purposes. When this heated water is returned to the river, it can raise the average temperature by 20 to 60 degrees. Although the water remains clean, raising the temperature creates *thermal pollution.* When the temperature of water increases, it loses its ability to hold oxygen, and that threatens fish and other animal life. Thermal water pollution affects reproductive behavior and alters the balance of marine populations. It may increase the growth of bacteria and algae, choking a waterway and causing a public health problem.

Besides damaging marine life, water pollution affects the source water from which *drinking water* must be processed. The quality of source water determines the ability, the process, and the expense required to produce safe, acceptable drinking water. In earlier days, when most of this country's water systems were designed, water treatment generally involved removing certain types of bacteria from relatively clean water. Today these systems are not able to cope with the increasing microbial problems and are generally ineffective against such new concerns as organic chemicals, trace metals, radioactive materials, and so on.

In order to insure a safe water supply, water is purified in treatment plants to remove chemical and biological impurities and to improve the appearance, taste, color, and odor.

2. Air Quality

Air pollution is the presence in the air of some impurity in great enough concentration to adversely affect health, safety, comfort, or enjoyment of property. Ralph Nader calls air pollution a new form of violence perpetrated against man, a form of "domestic chemical and biological warfare."

Most of the gases and particulates that man puts into the atmosphere are a result of combustion. The major products formed when coal and oil are burned are carbon dioxide and water. Although carbon dioxide (CO_2) may cause long-range climatic changes, it is not a serious pollutant, nor is the water. The air pollutants from combustion that are certainly dangerous are carbon monoxide (CO), sulfur dioxide (SO_2), nitrogen dioxide (NO_2), hydrocarbons, and suspended particulates.

Each year in the United States 200 million tons of fumes and soot are let loose into the air. That is about one ton of pollutant for each person. Fifty percent of that miasma comes from transportation vehicles, mainly automobiles. About 25 percent comes from the smokestacks of power-generating plants and boilers used to heat buildings. About 20 percent of this pollution is produced by industrial plants and factories that are refining petroleum, smelting iron, milling paper, synthesizing fabrics, and so on. About 2 percent comes from the burning of solid wastes.

COURTESY PHILLIPS PETROLEUM COMPANY
Industrial pollution darkens the sky.

Carbon monoxide, a deadly gas, is the leading single air pollutant, accounting for about half of the air pollutants by weight. Most carbon monoxide is produced by automobiles. Carbon monoxide combines with the blood, displacing the oxygen that the hemoglobin normally carries. When enough hemoglobin becomes tied up with carbon monoxide, the body starts to suffocate for lack of oxygen. Early symptoms include headache, loss of vision, nausea, abdominal pain, and decreased coordination. If the dosage is high enough and prolonged enough, death is the eventual result.

Nitrogen gas (N_2) and oxygen gas (O_2) exist in the atmosphere. When they are present in a car engine's cylinders during combustion, the high temperature and pressure cause some of the molecules to react to form nitrogen oxides. The most common nitrogen oxide produced is nitric oxide (NO), which reacts to form the very dangerous brown gas nitrogen dioxide (NO_2). NO_2 colors the air to the extent that you can see it in the smog of Los Angeles.

Besides smog and heavy traffic, Los Angeles also has a great deal of sunlight. When ultraviolet light from the sun strkes a molecule of NO_2, a free oxygen atom can be released. The free oxygen atom then can react with normal oxygen gas molecules (O_2) to form ozone (O_3). Ozone in the stratosphere is essential for life at the earth's surface. But a high concentration of ozone in the atmosphere of a city is a serious air pollutant. It reacts with other chemicals in the smog to produce strong oxidizing agents, which destroy the strength and elasticity of rubber, damage flowers, vegetables, and trees, and irritate the eyes and other susceptible membranes. Ozone and carbon monoxide are the principal culprits in the unhealthful air of urban areas.

When fossil fules containing sulfur are burned, sulfur oxides are emitted. Sulfur dioxide by itself is extremely irritating to the upper respiratory passages, even in very low concentrations. When the sulfur and nitrogen oxides combine with water droplets in the air, sulfuric, sulfurous, nitric, and nitrous acids are formed. When precipitation occurs, acid rain falls on the earth. The acid rain damages structures and upsets the ecological balance. Many streams have reached such acidic levels that fish can no longer survive. Also crops and wild vegetation depend on carefully buffered soil conditions, which are poisoned by the acid rain.

Particles in the air, such as soot, can put a heavy load on the capacity of the respiratory system to cleanse itself. It can also bring gaseous pollutants into the lungs by absorption. Other hazardous particles in the atmosphere are asbestos, beryllium, lead salts, mercury, and vinyl chloride. These can all lead to serious pulmonary disease.

Legislation and environmental protection programs on the Federal, state, and local levels have resulted in the formation of a new, rapidly expanding industry — the manufacture of pollution-control equipment. This industry is creating new jobs. Scientists and engineers are needed to design instruments for detecting pollutants and methods for controlling them.

3. Toxic Substance Control

Chemicals are invaluable to society, and most are believed relatively safe under normal conditions of use. But there are many chemicals whose environmental and health effects are unknown and some that have been proved harmful. *Toxic substances* are those that are poisonous or very hazardous to humans, animals, or plants.

Humans are exposed to toxic substances in a variety of ways — through the air they breathe, the water they drink, the food they eat, and the drugs, cosmetics, and other consumer products they use. The work-place, because of the concentration and duration of exposure to toxic chemicals, can be one of the most serious sources of exposure to them. The range of adverse human health effects of exposure to chemicals and other toxic substances is very broad. High-level exposures to some substances for even a short time may produce acute, though often temporary, effects such as rashes, burns, or poisoning. Prolonged exposure to low doses can cause chronic lung diseases, cancers, sterility, and other problems. There is growing evidence that toxic substances in the environment can cause reproductive problems, including miscarriages and birth defects.

The control of toxic substances in the environment is presenting a new challenge to the legal and regulatory system of the nation. With growing evidence of the human effects of some toxic substances, the number of lawsuits and other efforts to obtain compensation by injured parties appears to be rising.

Four Federal agencies deal with control of toxic substances — the Environmental Protection Agency, the Food and Drug Administration, the Occupational Health and Safety Administration, and the Consumer Product Safety Commission. These four agencies are now attempting to work together by sharing information and resources and by developing compatible testing procedures, research and development policies, and compliance procedures.

Implementation of toxic substance control laws will aid the government in protecting its citizens. The Federal Insecticide, Fungicide, and Rodenticide Act was passed to regulate the manufacture, sale, and use of pesticides and to protect consumers against harmful residues in food.

The Toxic Substances Control Act requires premarket screening of new and existing chemicals and provides for authority to require the testing of a chemical to determine its toxicity.

The transportation in commerce of hazardous materials by all modes of transportation is regulated by the Hazardous Transportation Act of 1974.

4. Noise Control

Noise has damaging effects: people become irritable, students have trouble studying, conversation is difficult, and the recuperative value of sleep is interfered with even when sleep is possible. Noise can raise blood pressure, heartbeat, and cholesterol levels. In addition, noise can permanently damage hearing. About 16 million Americans work on jobs where the noise level is so high that their hearing is in danger. Many of these 16 million are exposed to additional noise from traffic, demolition, and construction after they leave work.

Noise control is a relatively new and growing field, as more people become aware of the need for healthful surroundings. An increasing number of cities are adopting nuisance ordinances to prohibit certain noisy actions, such as operating construction equipment late at night, driving a car without a muffler, or disturbing neighbors by yelling or playing a radio too loud.

The National Environmental Policy Act (NEPA) requires that local and state governments assess the impact that proposed projects, such as highways, airports, and power plants, will have on the environment before they receive Federal funds. Noise engineers and noise-specialists now prepare environmental impact statements, predicting how much a new project will raise the noise level, so that excessive noise can be stopped before it begins.

5. Solid Waste Management

Solid waste management is in the midst of a transition from open and burning dumps to the disposal of waste through sanitary landfills. However, in the United States today, open dumping is still a major problem.

Health hazards are created by dumps through the presence of biological and chemical contaminants, which air, water, birds, insects, and rodents carry to people and domestic animals. In addition, dumps pollute both surface and groundwater, provide food and shelter for vermin, and disfigure the landscape.

A sanitary landfill can be designed and operated so that solid wastes can be disposed of on land under conditions that control odor, rodents, insects, and air and water pollution. In a sanitary landfill, solid waste is spread in thin layers, compacted to the smallest practical volume, and covered over in a manner that safeguards against pollution.

Many states and localities are investigating waste disposal systems that have a second purpose, the recovery of energy and other valuable resources. Some systems turn solid waste into steam that can turn a generator to produce electricity. Others are designed to turn the waste into a refined fuel that can be used to replace fossil fuel oil.

In 1965 the Federal Solid Waste Disposal Act initiated a research and development program for new and improved methods of solid waste disposal and provided technical and financial assistance to state and local governments. The Resource Conservation and Recovery Act of 1978 provides technical and financial assistance for the development of management plans, for facilities for the recovery of energy and other resources from discarded materials, for the safe disposal of discarded materials, and for regulation of the management of hazardous wastes.

B. ECOLOGY

In the natural world, organisms are challenged by physical and chemical fluctuations, predation (predators capturing and feeding on their prey), parasitism, and competition for resources. There are two methods by which species are able to survive — *genetic diversity* and *ecological diversity.*

Genetic diversity is the amount of difference among individuals in a single species. It maximizes the likelihood that at least some members of the species will withstand an environmental change. For example, the large number and variation among a single species of household roach usually allows some to be born with a resistance to a mild insecticide. Thus, when a homeowner sprays the chemical, most of the roaches die; however, some are immune, and the generations continue.

Ecological diversity, or *species richness,* is the term used to describe the variation and number of different species in a community of living things. The abundance of different organisms enhances the survival chances of the living community. The more food chains there are in an ecosystem, the more cross-connecting links there are among the food chains and the more chances there are for the ecosystem to compensate for changes imposed on it. A forest is far more stable during an environmental shift than a field of wheat.

Besides the aesthetic and humane reasons for seeking a harmonious relationship between all living organisms and the environment, many human and economic needs are served by preserving the natural balance.

In the next twenty years, the human population is expected to swell nearly 50 percent, and in some of the poorest countries nearly 100 percent. Demands on living resources will increase rapidly. If we continue to allow species to become extinct, certain special properties will expire with them. A tall, undistinguished-looking Mexican grass called teosinte could easily have disappeared from existence when weeds and shrubs were cleared for farmlands. This particular plant, however, when crossbred with corn, makes a corn mutant that tastes as good as corn but is perennial. Regular corn must be replanted every year, whereas this new species will regrow from its underground stems every year. It is also more virus-resistant and can grow in a greater variety of soils. The teosinte could easily have become extinct before its value was discovered. Only a few thousand of the plants existed. The new species of corn produced from it may save the world multibillions of dollars, provide food, and require less energy for its cultivation.

Scientists are currently researching many rare plant and animal species that can help the world's food supply. They are also examining plants that can be used for energy. Giant kelp, a fast-growing seaweed, can yield methane (natural gas) for industrial and home use. Scientists are experimenting with certain species of fast-growing cottonwood trees, which not only can be burned as fuel but also enrich the soil with nitrogen.

Some plants have unique chemical properties. A great deal of rubber is made synthetically from oil, but research on latex-bearing tropical plants may bring down the price of natural rubber so that the oil can be used in other ways. The jojoba plant, found in the desert, yields a lubricant almost as good as that produced by the sperm whale. In the future, jojoba farming may make sperm whale killing unprofitable.

Plants, fungi, insects, and certain species of marine invertebrates contain chemicals that make powerful pharmaceuticals. Penicillin and erythromycin are antibiotics made from plants. These drugs kill bacterial cells but do not harm human cells. Other animal and plant chemicals are being looked at as possible cancer cures or inhibitors. More than 500 species of marine animals and over 2,500 species of plants have been found that produce chemicals known to have anticancer activity.

C. LAND MANAGEMENT

The nation has long been proud of the richness and diversity of its soil, water, and mineral resources and of its ability to convert these resources into food, fiber, and other marketable products. We have also given increasing attention to the recreational, aesthetic, cultural, and scientific value of these resources in their natural state — as forests, rivers, mountains, and grasslands replete with fish and other wildlife.

Conflicts among these competing uses of the nation's natural resources have intensified as people have begun to recognize both the economic and environmental limits of resource exploitation. There are persistent problems in the use of natural resources, such as overgrazing of rangeland, erosion of topsoil, depletion of groundwater, loss of wetlands and wildlife, and the increasing scarcity of fossil fuels and other minerals, which are not amenable to short-term or isolated solution. Rather, longer-range integrated efforts are needed to achieve more efficient management and use of these resources while maintaining environmental quality.

Some conflicts between resource protection and resource development are unavoidable, but in some areas, notably agriculture, the management strategies that are evolving appear to have both economic and environmental benefits.

One of the most serious environmental problems facing U.S. agriculture today is soil erosion. More than 140 million acres (one-third of the U.S. cropland base) are eroding at serious rates. This impact is marked in part by the intensive agricultural use of energy in the form of fertilizers and pesticides. Such practices raise crop yields but result in pollution problems when these materials or their breakdown products are washed or blown from the fields. Scientists, citizens, and Federal regulatory agencies continue to debate the net social benefits of some pesticides, animal growth stimulants, irrigation projects, and alternative management approaches that rely on natural biological cycles.

Basic research on environmentally sound yet productive agricultural systems follows many avenues — enhancing the photosynthetic efficiency of plants, breeding the capability to affix nitrogen into cereal crops, developing multiple cropping systems, and discovering more reliable methods to control crop pests. Recently, research has been very favorable in an analysis of alternative farming methods that use various combinations of tillage practices, cropping patterns, fertilizers, and pesticides.

Controversy and tensions over how public lands should be managed are increasing. Of the 2.3 billion acres of land within the United States, the Federal government manages approximately one-third — 775.2 million acres. About one-half is in Alaska, and about 90 percent of the rest is in eleven Western states. These lands are a vast storehouse of natural resources and values. Competition among supporters of grazing, mining, outdoor recreation, fish and wildlife, timber, water supplies, and wilderness is intense.

The growth in demand for natural resources — energy, minerals, and timber — concurrent with rising concern for the quality of the environment and with emphasis on protection, preservation, and nonexploitative uses, has generated increasing conflict. To address these issues, the Congress has passed several major statutes relating to public land management. These statutes established the principle that the management of federally managed forests and rangelands would be based on detailed inventories of the resources, careful planning, and public participation, with the goal of achieving a balance among competing uses.

D. ENERGY

The United States is an industrialized nation that consumes a huge amount of energy to maintain its high standard of living. In the technologically advanced nations, the energy consumed is not merely to meet basic needs, but to run its appliance-laden households, its industries, and its transportation. Although our population amounts to only 7 percent of the world's population, we use about one-third of the world's energy!

About 95 percent of our energy today comes from the burning of *fossil fuels.* The fossil fuels are *coal, natural gas,* and *petroleum* (gasoline, diesel fuel, and heating oil primarily). They are called fossil fuels because they are all derived from prehistoric plants that have been buried within the crust of the earth for millions of years. Heat and pressure turned this once living material, which stored the sun's energy in its cells, into today's fuels. Of course, once the coal, petroleum, or natural gas is burned, it cannot be used again. These fossil fuels are thus called *nonrenewable fuels.* Within the next century, most of the gas and oil deposits will be exhausted and the remainder of coal will be greatly reduced.

In a peculiar way, the energy crisis, which was brought about by economic pressures from foreign governments, has shocked the United States into a realization of the benefits of energy conservation. The United States is heading in a new direction toward the more efficient and thoughtful use of energy. There are now auto efficiency standards requiring that all cars have an average city mileage rate of 27.5 miles per gallon of gasoline by 1985. The 55 mph speed limit not only saves fuel, but also saves lives.

Tax credits are being given to homeowners and commercial enterprises for making their properties more energy-efficient, such as by the installation of thermal-pane storm windows, fiberglass insulation, and solar heating pumps. The National Energy Act even requires that home appliances, such as refrigerators and air conditioners, be made more energy-efficient.

Within the next few decades it is hoped that renewable energy sources will be developed. We have already discussed the research involving kelp and cottonwood as fuel. Another *biomass* project involves the production of alcohol from grain, which can be efficiently burned in internal combustion engines. The earth itself offers renewable energy resources. For hundreds of years falling water and the wind have been used by man. Soon we may be using the heat energy that produces geysers and volcanoes, as well as the waves and tidal action of the oceans, to generate electricity for our homes and factories.

The solar battery is a device that converts the energy of sunlight directly into electricity. Currently it would cost about $750 in solar battery cells to light one light bulb, but soon the price will come down, and solar batteries may become a practical source of power.

Nuclear energy is a source of heat and radiation that can be used for peaceful as well as military purposes. Although peaceful applications have been expanding rapidly in recent years, they are still in the early stages of development. Continuing research and development programs will be needed during the next several decades to find newer, safer, and more efficient ways of utilizing this energy.

When nuclear energy is used commercially for power, the heat generated is converted to electricity. Because of the potential hazards of nuclear radiation, special radiation-resistant materials are used in reactors, and extensive safety measures are taken to protect personnel. Nuclear reactors have become competitive with systems that use fossil fuels. In 1979 there were 72 nuclear reactors in commercial operation, with about 134 in the planning stage. Dual-purpose nuclear-power desalting plants, which would provide at the same time a new source of fresh water and electric power, are being studied.

E. ENVIRONMENTAL SCIENCE

Environmental science helps us understand our natural environment — the earth, its atmosphere, and the oceans. This field, sometimes known as earth science, is concerned with the history, composition, and characteristics of the earth's surface, interior, and atmosphere. Basic research in environmental science increases our scientific knowledge, whereas applied work uses the knowledge gained from the basic research for solving practical problems. Environmental science plays an important role in solving environmental pollution problems.

Geology involves the study of the structure, composition, and history of the earth's crust. By examining surface rocks and drilling to recover rock cores, geologists determine the types and distribution of rocks beneath the earth's surface. They conduct geological surveys, draw maps, take measurements, and record data. Geological research helps to determine the structure and history of the earth and may result in significant advances, such as the ability to predict earthquakes. An important application of geologists' work is locating oil and other minerals.

Geophysics is the study of the composition and physical aspects of the earth and its electric, magnetic, and gravitational fields. Solid earth geophysicists search for oil and mineral deposits, map the earth's surface, and study earthquakes. Exploration geophysicists use seismic prospecting techniques to locate oil and mineral deposits. Geodesists study the size, shape, and gravitational fields of the earth and other planets. Their principal task is to make the precise measurements necessary for accurate mapping of the earth's surface. Hydrologists study the distribution of underground and surface waters, including rivers, glaciers, snow, and permafrost.

Meteorology is the scientific study of the atmosphere. Meteorologists try to understand the atmosphere's physical characteristics, motions, and processes. They attempt to determine the ways in which the atmosphere affects the rest of our physical environment. The best-known application of meteorology is the forecasting of weather. Meteorological research also is used in solving air pollution problems and in studying trends in the earth's climate.

Oceanography uses the principles and techniques of natural science, mathematics, and engineering to study oceans. Oceanographers investigate the sea's movements, physical properties, and plant and animal life. Their research not only extends basic scientific knowledge, but also helps develop practical methods for forecasting weather, developing fisheries, mining ocean resources, and improving national defense.

Chapter **III**

Skills, Schooling, and Environmental Careers

In this chapter we shall investigate your qualifications. There are exercises that will help you examine your work values and interests. You will discover if you share interests with environmentalists. You will be able to compare your abilities with the professional and personal characteristics of people working in several environmental occupations. You will achieve a picture of yourself and perhaps be better able to define your lifetime career goals.

This chapter also discusses the role of schooling in preparation for a job in the environment. The last sections will tell you how you should start your training in high school for an environmental career.

A. CHOOSING A CAREER

Before choosing a career in the environmental field, you should consider a few questions. What do you enjoy doing? What are you good at? How much education do you plan to get? How much money can you spend on training? What special talents do you have? What special skills do you have? How well do you do in school? Are there any jobs available in the occupations that most interest you?

The career you choose is likely to affect many aspects of your life. It may influence where you will live, how much money you will have to spend, whether you can easily raise a family, your position in the community, and so on. When you choose a career, you are directly or indirectly making decisions about the types of people you would like to work with, the amount of leisure time you want, and the importance of money in your life.

There are environmental careers where you will be a kind of policeman protecting our natural resources. There are fields where you will be working on pure science research problems, such as trying to turn coal into petroleum or trying to find a sexual lure that will attract a pest away from a crop. You may be involved in planning and building a safer nuclear energy plant. You may be a designer, developing a wildlife refuge where no commercial development can occur. Or you may be a craftsman, using your skills and training to build a safer, healthier world.

How do you know what jobs are best for you? Howard E. Figler, Director of Counseling at Dickinson College, developed a list of 33 "satisfactions" people get from their jobs.[1] First read the entire list. As you do, look carefully at the definitions of each "satisfaction." How important are these things to you? Then go over the list again. This time, rate each item on the list, using the scale below.

> 1 = Not important at all
> 2 = Not very important
> 3 = Reasonably important
> 4 = Very important

Work Values Exercise

---

1. _____ *Help society:* Contribute to the betterment of the world I live in.

2. _____ *Help others:* Help other people directly, either individually or in small groups.

3. _____ *Public contact:* Have a lot of day-to-day contact with people.

4. _____ *Work with others:* Have close working relationships with a group; work as a team toward common goals.

5. _____ *Affiliation:* Be recognized as a member of an organization whose type of work or status is important to me.

6. _____ *Friendship:* Develop close personal relationships with the people I work with.

7. _____ *Competition:* Pit my abilities against others. There are clear outcomes.

8. _____ *Make decisions:* Have the power to set policy and determine a course of action.

9. _____ *Work under pressure:* Work in a situation where deadlines and high quality work are required by my supervisor.

10. _____ *Power and authority:* Control other people's work activities.

11. _____ *Influence people:* Be in a position to change other people's attitudes and opinions.

12. _____ *Work alone:* Do things by myself, without much contact with others.

13. _____ *Knowledge:* Seek knowledge, truth, and understanding.

14. _____ *Intellectual status:* Be regarded by others as a person of intellectual achievement or an expert.

15. _____ *Artistic creativity:* Do creative work in any of several art forms.

16. _____ *Creativity (general):* Create new ideas, programs, organizational structures, or anything else that has not been developed by others.

17. _____ *Aesthetics:* Have a job that involves sensitivity to beauty.

18. _____ *Supervision:* Have a job in which I guide other people in their work.

19. _____ *Change and variety:* Have job duties that often change or are done in different settings.

20. _____ *Precision work:* Do work that allows little tolerance for error.

21. _____ *Stability:* Have job duties that are largely predictable and not likely to change over a long period of time.

22. _____ *Security:* Be assured of keeping my job and a reasonable financial reward.

23. _____ *Fast pace:* Work quickly; keep up with a fast pace.

24. _____ *Recognition:* Be recognized for the quality of my work in some visible or public way.

25. _____ *Excitement:* Do work that is very exciting or that often is exciting.

26. _____ *Adventure:* Do work that requires me to take risks.

27. _____ *Profit, gain:* Expect to earn large amounts of money or other material possessions.

28. _____ *Independence:* Decide for myself what kind of work I'll do and how I'll go about it; not have to do what others tell me to do.

---

[1]Bureau of Labor Statistics, *Exploring Careers,* Bulletin 2001, p. 5-6.

29. _____ *Moral fulfillment:* Feel that my work is contributing to a set of moral standards that I feel are very important.

30. _____ *Location:* Find a place to live (town, geographic area) that matches my life-style and allows me to do the things I enjoy most.

31. _____ *Community:* Live in a town or city where I can get involved in community affairs.

32. _____ *Physical challenge:* Have a job whose physical demands are challenging and rewarding.

33. _____ *Time freedom:* Handle my job according to my own time schedule; no specific working hours required.

Now that you have rated each of these work values, look over your list. Select those that mean the most to you and list them on a separate piece of paper. If you can think of any other things that are very important to you, add them to your list.

What do these work values tell you about yourself? If you consider each one as a piece of a puzzle and then start trying to fit them together, the picture of an individual may begin to emerge — a picture of you.

B. SHOULD I BE AN ENVIRONMENTALIST?

Answer the following questions with Yes or No:

1. Do you like nature?
2. Do you like challenges?
3. Do you like hard work?
4. Do you like science?
5. Do you like mathematics?
6. Do you like to find out how things work (a car, a TV, a toaster)?
7. Are you interested in plants and animals?
8. Are you interested in the weather?
9. When you go to the seashore, do you think about the ocean, the shore, the seaweed, and the marine life?
10. Do you try to conserve energy and water in your household?

11. Do you like going to the zoo and natural history museums?

12. Do you like watching nature and science programs on television?

13. Have you read and enjoyed many nature or science books?

14. Do you subscribe to a nature or science magazine?

15. Do you belong to a science club?

16. Can you read a map easily?

17. Do you like games with lots of rules?

18. Are you generally able to avoid frustration if situations become confusing?

19. Can you argue effectively without becoming mean?

20. Do you like to use tools?

21. If you have a problem, do you prefer figuring it out yourself to having someone else give you the answer?

22. Do you mind working alone?

23. Do you like working with others?

24. Do you keep your room rather neat, or at least orderly?

25. Do you turn in your school assignments on time?

26. Do you like helping other people?

27. Does littering annoy you?

28. Do you like to study?

29. Do you have the patience to do something many times until you get it right?

30. Do you like mysteries or mysterious ideas?

31. Can you work in a unstructured situation?

32. Do you ask a lot of questions until you are satisfied that you understand a problem or new idea?

33. Do you think computers are a benefit to mankind?

34. Do you sometimes challenge the ideas and attitudes of others?

35. Do you usually finish what you start?

36. Money is not the only reason for a job?

37. Often there are two or more sides to a problem?

38. One of the main reasons you go to school is because you like to learn.

39. Are you usually cooperative at home and at school?

40. Do you sometimes like to sit quietly and think?

If most of your answers were Yes, then perhaps you would be happy in an environmental career.

C. ENVIRONMENTAL CAREER CATEGORIES

There are many careers involving the environment. Some require a bachelor's degree or higher, some require special training or a two-year community college degree, and some require special craft skills and abilities. There are environmental jobs where you work in a laboratory, there are some where you work outdoors, some in an office, and some at an industrial plant. Some require hard, rigorous physical work, while others require a lot of quiet thinking. Good communications skills are needed for some careers, and good clerical skills are needed for others.

I have divided 155 careers in the environment into four categories.

The Category I jobs are science careers that involve working with and protecting the environment. All require a minimum of four years of college, and for many of them you may also have to take graduate training before you can be hired.

The Category II jobs are technician-level careers that usually require specialized training in a two-year community college program, or a technical school.

The Category III careers generally require apprenticeship or vocational school training. Category III jobs often require a talent for working with tools and machinery.

Category IV jobs are highly specialized careers, which generally require training beyond the bachelor's degree as well as certain talents and abilities.

Category I: Scientific and Engineering Careers Involving the Environment

A. Chemists
   1. Water purification chemist
   2. Wastewater treatment chemist
   3. Air chemist
   4. Industrial waste chemist
   5. Agricultural chemist
   6. Toxicologist
   7. Colloid chemist
   8. Geochemist
   9. Polymer chemist
   10. Synthetic chemist

11. Radiochemist
12. Analytical instrumentation chemist
13. Pathological chemist
14. Metallurgical chemist
15. Electrochemist
16. Nuclear chemist
17. Photochemist
18. Radiation chemist
19. Structural chemist
20. Surface chemist

B. Physicists
1. Solid state physicist
2. Nuclear physicist
3. Acoustical physicist
4. Thermophysicist
5. Electrophysicist
6. Magnetophysicist

C. Life Scientists
1. Agricultural services biologist
2. Agronomist
3. Plant anatomist
4. Plant biochemist
5. Plant geneticist
6. Plant pathologist
7. Horticulturist
8. Entomologist
9. Microbiologist
10. Pathologist
11. Environmental epidemiologist
12. Fish biologist
13. Wildlife biologist
14. Ecologist
15. Biosociologist
16. Biogeographer
17. Limnologist
18. Marine biologist
19. Biometeorologist
20. Zoologist

21. Animal husbandry specialist
22. Biochemist
23. Pharmacologist
24. Food scientist
25. Biometrician

D. Environmental Engineer
1. Sanitary engineer
2. Hydrologic engineer
3. Water pollution control engineer
4. Industrial water treatment engineer
5. Petroleum engineer
6. Oil pollution control engineer
7. Mining engineer
8. Nuclear engineer
9. Noise engineer
10. Air engineer
11. Agricultural engineer
12. Waste management engineer
13. Resource recovery engineer

E. Environmental Scientist
1. Geologist
2. Mineralogist
3. Petrologist
4. Economic geologist
5. Marine geologist
6. Geochemist
7. Geothermal geologist
8. Geomorphologist
9. Petroleum geologist
10. Engineering geologist
11. Geophysicist
12. Solid earth geophysicist
13. Fluid earth geophysicist
14. Upper atmosphere geophysicist
15. Geodesist
16. Seismologist
17. Geomagnetic physicist
18. Paleomagnetic physicist

19. Volcanologist
20. Hydrologist
21. Technophysicist
22. Exploration geophysicist
23. Meteorologist
24. Physical meteorologist
25. Climatologist
26. Air pollution meteorologist

27. Biometeorologist
28. Paleoclimatologist
29. Oceanographer
30. Physical oceanographer
31. Chemical oceanographer
32. Geological oceanographer
33. Biological oceanographer
34. Fish scientist or aquaculturist

F. Conservation Scientist

1. Forester
2. Range manager
3. Soil conservationist

Category II: Environmental Technician-Level Careers

A. Water treatment plant operator
B. Wastewater treatment plant operator
C. Wastewater treatment plant laboratory technician
D. Water treatment plant laboratory technician
E. Water pollution control technician
F. Estuarine resource technician
G. Water and sewer drafter
H. Audiometrist
I. Noise technician
J. Air technician
K. Meteorological technician
L. Fish culturist
M. Forestry technician
N. Chemical laboratory technician
O. Engineering technician
P. Radiation laboratory technician
Q. Radiation monitor

Category III: Environmental Skilled Crafts Careers

A. Water treatment plant mechanic
B. Industrial waste inspector

    C. Photo-inspection technician
    D. Canal tender
    E. Watershed tender
    F. Noise pollution assistant
    G. Air pollution assistant
    H. Conservation officer
    I. Forestry assistant
    J. Park ranger
    K. Entomology field assistant
    L. Vector control assistant (epidemiological assistant)
    M. Mining and petroleum operatives and craft workers
        1. Oil well driller
        2. Mining machine operator
        3. Mining and oil drilling mechanic
        4. Pumper
        5. Gauger
        6. Engine worker
    N. Petroleum refinery operator
    O. Electric power plant operator
        1. Electrician
        2. Instrument repairer
        3. Industrial machinery repairer
        4. Machinist
        5. Pipe fitter
        6. Welder
        7. Boilermaker
    P. Nuclear power plant operator
        1. Drafter
        2. Radiation monitor
        3. Nuclear machinist
        4. Chemical process operator

Category IV: Other Environmental Careers

    A. Land planner
    B. Land architect
    C. Environmental economist
    D. Environmental lawyer
    E. Environmental lobbyist
    F. Occupational health physician
    G. Occupational health nurse

D. JOB CHARACTERISTICS

There are a number of job characteristics that are helpful when you are selecting an occupation. Here is a list of fifteen. As you read them, consider those that describe a condition that suits your interests, talents, and personality. If you find that any are particularly annoying or disagreeable, you certainly do not want to spend your life in a career requiring that attribute.

For instance, it is possible to be an oceanographer and avoid sea voyages, but it is unlikely. If you do not want to be indoors all day long, you should not be a chemical technician. If you like working with your hands and you do not want to go to school after high school, then you might be a conservation officer. An artistic talent could help you find a career as a landscape architect. Good problem-solving skills are necessary for the engineering careers, and so on.

Problem-solving ability — the ability to identify a problem and decide what should be done to correct it. All Category I and Category IV jobs require a high degree of this skill. Technicians and craft workers, too, may be more successful if they have this ability, but it is generally not a requirement for employment.

Use of tools, machinery — takes a talent for working with your hands. Often, knowing how machines work is necessary, too. This skill is usually necessary for Category III jobs and is very helpful for jobs in Categories I and II.

Instruction of others — the ability to help others learn to do or understand something. Category IV professionals usually need this skill, and many jobs in the environmental industries require that you be able to explain rules and regulations clearly to others, as well as to persuade people to follow your way of thinking.

Repetitious work — work in which the same thing is done over and over again. Category II and III jobs usually require that you perform essentially the same task over and over again. However, most environmental jobs are not nearly so repetitive as assembly line work, since the worker is often involved in new situations or locales.

Hazardous work — involves the use of dangerous equipment or materials or work in dangerous surroundings. Some wilderness career jobs, those involving the energy industry, and some of the scientific occupations have some element of risk, although the dangers are usually carefully monitored and under control.

Outdoor work — refers to occupations in which a major portion of time is spent outdoors, frequently without regard to weather conditions. Most environmental jobs are in plants, laboratories, and office buildings, but some require considerable time outdoors, such as range manager, park ranger, oceanographer, the agricultural professions, and the forestry fields.

Generally confined work — workers have to stay in one place most of the time. People who work at a laboratory bench, a desk, or a computer terminal are examples.

Physical stamina — ability to lift heavy weights, walk long distances, stand for long periods, or stoop frequently. Many of the Category III occupations require physical stamina and endurance.

Precision — work involves high standards of accuracy. All careers in the environmental fields generally require this skill.

Work with detail — refers to technical data, numbers, or written specifications. Category I, II, and IV jobs require this ability.

Creativity — work involves new ideas, programs, designs, or products. Success in the Category I jobs, the sciences, often requires good imagination. Some Category V jobs, too, require this talent.

Influence on others — the ability to stimulate others to think or act in a certain way. Teachers, lawyers, and lobbyists (Category IV) are successful if they possess this ability.

Work as part of a team — refers to occupations in which cooperation with co-workers is an integral part of the job. All of the environmental professions require this capability.

Jobs widely scattered — occupations that are found in most parts of the country. Most technical and scientific jobs are located around large metropolitan areas. Of course, agricultural and wilderness occupations are rural. Jobs with energy companies are generally located near large cities; however, those that deal with discovery of resources may require living in remote or foreign areas.

Initiative — jobs that demand the ability to determine on one's own what should be done, as well as the motivation to do it without close supervision. This skill is required by people who want careers in Categories I and IV.

E. MATCHING PERSONAL AND JOB CHARACTERISTICS

Now that you know something about your personal work values and also a little about certain job characteristics, let us examine some environmental careers and discover whether they are right for you.

Environmental Engineering
1. What kind of work might you do?
   a) Establish computational methods and computer input data to analyze problems in design.

b. Apply knowledge of properties of various materials to the development of more energy-efficient machines.

c) Design facilities and equipment for a water purification plant.

d) Analyze technical and cost factors to plan methods to recover oil and gas.

e) Investigate safety features at a nuclear power plant and recommend design changes.

2. What skills and abilities do you need for this kind of work? You must be able to:

a) Use high-level mathematics.

b) Understand principles of chemistry, geology, physics, and related sciences.

c) Solve problems, using facts and personal judgment.

d) Work on different projects and with changing situations.

e) Deal with various kinds of people.

EXXON PHOTO

A chemical engineer oversees a petroleum refinery.

3. How do you know if you would like or could learn to do this kind of work?

a) Have you read mechanical or automotive design magazines? Do you enjoy and understand technical articles?

b) Have you taken courses in algebra, geometry, and advanced math? Can you solve practical problems using math?

c) Have you built a model airplane, an automobile, or a bridge? Can you look at a blueprint or drawing and visualize the final structure?

    d) Have you taken physics courses? Do you like to study energy and matter?

    e) Have you built or repaired a radio, a television set, or an amplifier? Do you understand electrical or electronic terms and drawings?

4. How can you prepare for this type of work?

Four to five years of college leading to a bachelor's degree in education is the minimum requirement for a job. Most engineering schools require an above-average record in mathematics, physics, chemistry, and English.

5. What else should you consider about these jobs?

Many engineers work under quiet conditions in modern offices and research laboratories. Others work in mines, factories, at construction sites, or at outdoor locations.

Engineering Technician

1. What kind of work might you do?

    a) Use astronomical observations, complex computations, and other techniques to compile data for preparing geodetic maps and charts for oil exploration.

    b) Organize and direct the work of surveying parties to determine precise location and measurement points.

    c) Use drafting instruments to prepare detailed drawings and blueprints for a sewer system.

    d) Prepare detailed working drawings of a newly designed engine showing dimensions, tolerances, and other engineering data.

    e) Direct activities of workers who set seismographic recording instruments and gather data about oil-bearing rock layers.

2. What skills and abilities do you need for this kind of work? You must be able to:

    a) Use geometry and other kinds of higher mathematics.

    b) Perform detail work with great accuracy.

    c) Use fingers skillfully when making drawings.

    d) Be able to operate equipment, adjust instruments, use a pen to make sketches, or use measuring tools.

    d) Make decisions according to both personal judgment and facts.

    e) Direct activities of other workers.

    f) Work with a team.

    g) Perform under stress in emergency situations.

3. How do you know if you would like or could learn to do this kind of work?

    a) Have you taken courses in mechanical drawing? Do you enjoy this type of activity?

b) Have you taken courses in geometry and advanced math? Do you like math studies?
c) Have you made models of airplanes or cars following detailed plans? Can you follow instructions well?
d) Have you taken courses in physics or chemistry? Can you work with formulas?
4. How can you prepare for this type of work?

Occupations in this group usually require technical, vocational, or community college coursework in mathematics, physical sciences, industrial arts, and mechanical drawing. Technicians usually begin work as trainees in routine jobs under close supervision of an experienced technician or engineer. As they gain experience, they move up to jobs requiring less supervision.

Physical Scientist
1. What kind of work might you do?
a) Study aerial photographs for indications of oil and gas deposits.
b) Examine rock formations to develop theories about the earth and its history.
c) Use information about wind, temperature, humidity, and land formations to predict weather.
d) Trace pollutants dumped in wastewater from factories.
e) Develop chemicals and processes for less polluting manufacture.
f) Conduct experiments to develop new materials.
g) Analyze new energy processes.
h) Gather and interpret information about the earth.
i) Use computers and advanced mathematics to solve complex environmental problems.

2. What skills and abilities do you need for this kind of work? You must be able to:
a) Use logic or scientific thinking to deal with many different kinds of problems.
b) Use nonverbal symbols (such as numbers) to express ideas or solve problems.
c) Understand and express complex, technical, and scientific information.
d) Recognize textures, colors, shapes, and sizes.
e) Make decisions using your own judgment.
f) Gather and interpret data.
g) Make decisions based on information that can be measured or verified.

3. How do you know if you would like or could learn to do this kind of work?

   a) Have you taken courses in earth science, chemistry, or physics? Did you enjoy these courses?
   b) Have you read articles or stories about scientific discoveries or expeditions?
   c) Do you understand scientific terminology?
   d) Have you collected rocks or minerals as a hobby?
   e) Have you watched science shows on television? Do you understand the terms and symbols they use?
   f) Have you owned a chemistry set or microscope? Do you enjoy testing new ideas with this type of equipment?
4. How can you prepare for this kind of work?

   A bachelor's degree is the minimum requirement for a scientist. Many careers require a master's or doctorate for employment. Important high school preparation courses are biology, chemistry, physics, algebra, trigonometry, and English.

EXXON PHOTO

Chemists conduct experiments to develop new materials.

Life Scientist
1. What kind of work might you do?
   a) Prepare slides and use microscopes to study cells and cell structure.
   b) Examine animals and specimens to study the effects of pollution and chemicals on living tissue.
   c) Conduct experiments with growing microorganisms.
   d) Study the origin and classification of plants or animals.
   e) Study the habitat and life functions of plants or animals.

f) Conduct experiments by breeding animals or plants.
g) Conduct research to develop improved methods to raise domesticated plants or animals.

2. What skills and abilities do you need for this kind of work? You must be able to:
   a) Use logic and scientific methods to study living things.
   b) Understand instructions that use words, numbers, diagrams, or chemical formulas.
   c) Learn and use knowledge about how living things function, how plants and animals are classified, and how to use laboratory and scientific equipment.
   d) Recognize differences in size, form, shape, color, and texture.
   e) Use eyes, hands, and fingers easily and accurately.
   f) Do a lot of different things and change what you are doing frequently.
   g) Make decisions using your own judgment.
   h) Make decisions based on information that can be measured or verified.
   i) Do things that require you to be very careful and accurate.

3. How do you know if you would like or could learn to do this kind of work?
   a) Have you studied plants in a garden, forest, or greenhouse? Can you recognize and identify different types of plants?
   b) Have you participated in a project or hobby that involved breeding, caring for, or studying plant or animal life?
   c) Have you taken courses in biology or zoology? Do you enjoy conducting experiments that involve plants or animals?
   d) Have you been a member of a scouting or environmental protection group? Do you take part in efforts to preserve forests, parks, or a city's environment?

4. How can you prepare for this kind of work?
   A bachelor's degree with a major in biology or another science is generally required. Graduate degrees are needed for most research work or for college teaching. A master's degree may qualify for laboratory work, but a PhD is usually needed.

Laboratory Technician
1. What kind of work might you do?
   a) Set up and operate laboratory equipment to conduct chemical and physical tests on environmental samples.
   b) Prepare slides and use microscopes to identify diseases in an organ removed by surgery.

c) Measure rainfall and riverflow, record findings, and prepare a summary report of conditions.

d) Set up equipment to test an engine to gather evidence for pollution control.

e) Prepare compounds and package chemicals for fertilizing fields.

f) Conduct tests on samples from oil drilling operations.

g) Run a fish hatchery.

1. What skills and abilities do you need for this kind of work? You must be able to:

a) Understand and use scientific and technical language and symbols.

b) Recognize slight differences in the shape, color, or texture of things.

c) Use eyes, hands, and fingers to operate delicate and sensitive equipment.

d) Do work that requires being very precise or accurate.

e) Follow technical instructions that may be verbal, written, or in the form of charts or drawings.

f) Use measurable and verifiable information for making decisions or judgments.

3. How do you know if you would like or could learn to do this kind of work?

a) Have you used test tubes, microscopes, or other laboratory instruments? Do you enjoy working with scientific equipment?

b) Have you read scientific or technical magazines? Can you understand the language and symbols used?

c) Have you collected rocks or insects? Can you recognize different minerals in the rocks or species of insects?

d) Have you taken courses in algebra or geometry? Can you read and understand charts and graphs?

e) Have you repaired a precision device such as a radio, a clock, or an automobile?

4. How can you prepare for this kind of work?

Many laboratory technician jobs require training after high school in a technical, vocational, or community college. Some workers may move into laboratory work from unskilled production areas. On-the-job training is sometimes available to applicants who have appropriate skills or experience.

F. SCHOOL AND WORK

The first step in choosing a career is discovering some things about yourself. We have mentioned that different jobs suit different kinds of people. The right career for you depends on the person you really are, or want to be.

You have completed the work values exercise. You may have a clearer picture now of your reasons for working, and a better idea of the things about a job that matter to you.

The table on personal and job characteristics may have helped you narrow down the occupational categories to those that appeal to you most. You also have examined five general careers.

Now let us look at the relationship between school and choosing an environmental career. First, decide what your favorite subject is. Then list the subjects that come easily for you. Place a check next to those subjects on your list that you find interesting. (Try to leave out the personalities of your teachers.)

Preparing for many of the careers in the environment involves studying and enjoying science. Some science courses should be on your list, and hopefully there should be a check next to them.

Mathematics, too, is very important in most of the environmental fields. Agriculture, energy, forestry, fishery, health, environmental protection, and all scientific and technical occupations rely on good mathematical skills. Math may not be a favorite course of yours, but you should be comfortable with learning and using it. More and more environmental careers depend on computers for collecting data and for helping environmentalists understand current problems and find ways for seeking solutions.

Business education skills are very helpful in the energy, agricultural, and conservation-related occupations. Business skills, as well as understanding of politics and history, are important if you want to help develop our country's resources and protect them.

English and language arts courses, such as speech, are very useful for persuading other people of the necessity for carrying out new environmentally sound designs. Conservationists argue in books, in magazine articles, on talk shows, and in newspapers about the merits of their proposals. Scientific work and craft work, too, require writing and speaking skills in order to pass along information, ideas, and results.

If you like your shop and industrial arts courses, you may be able to find a career in the craft, technical, or scientific fields where you will be working with tools, machines, and electronic equipment to study nature or to provide energy for the nation.

How well you do in school is also important in choosing a career. The Category I and Category IV jobs require at least a bachelor's degree. You need not be a genius to be a productive and successful scientist or engineer, but the competition for jobs is keen, and your classwork grades are a good indication of how bright you are and how hard you work. You need not be a "straight A" student, but if you are getting a lot of C's, particularly in science and math courses, perhaps your abilities are in other areas.

If you can graduate from high school and want to work in an environmental career, but four-year colleges are not for you, then you should consider one of the technical careers listed in Category II. These jobs usually require community college training. They are interesting and very helpful in protecting and wisely using our resources. You work with highly trained specialists who tell you what measurements, experiments, tests, or activities are needed.

There are jobs involving the environment that require no college. If you are good with tools or machines, there are many careers that can use your skills. Running and maintaining water purification plants, oil refineries, and waste disposal plants require many skilled craft workers. Normally, apprenticeship programs or vocational schools provide the training you need for these jobs.

Another important factor to consider about choosing a career that requires four, six, or eight years of schooling beyond high school is cost. You have to think about how much training you or your family can afford as well as how much you would like to obtain. Keep in mind, though, that there are many sources of financial aid. Do not be discouraged if you have the ability and interest to pursue education or training after high school but your family cannot afford the cost. Scholarships, loans, grants, and other financial aids are available from schools, educational foundations, business firms, religious groups, community organizations, and Federal, state, and local governments.

Another way to prepare for a job is to join the Armed Forces. The Armed Forces train people in many technical occupations. You can learn job skills and gain work experience while you are in the service and then, when you complete your tour of duty, use those skills to get a civilian job. Special benefits and programs can help you finance training at a vocational or technical school, or at a college.

G. SOURCES OF FINANCIAL AID INFORMATION

If possible, consult a high school guidance counselor or college financial aid officer for advice on sources of financial aid. Don't neglect any possibility, for many organizations offer scholarships, fellowships, grants, loans, and work-study programs. Study the many directories and guides to sources of student financial aid which are updated and revised periodically and are generally available in guidance offices and public libraries. Many career information systems also provide information on financial aid.

The Federal government provides several kinds of financial assistance to needy students: grants, loans, work-study, and benefits. Details are presented in a pamphlet entitled *Student Consumer's Guide; Six Federal Financial Aid Programs, 1979-80*. This pamphlet is frequently revised; request the current edition from:

Bureau of Student Financial Assistance, Post Office Box 84, Washington, DC 20044.

Some student aid programs are designed to assist specific groups: Hispanics, blacks, native Americans, or women, for example. *Selected List of Postsecondary Education Opportunities for Minorities and Women,* published annually by the U.S. Department of Education, is a useful guide to organizations that offer loan, scholarship, and fellowship assistance, with special emphasis on aids for minorities and women. Opportunities for financial aid are listed by fields of study, including engineering, science, and health. Educational opportunities with the Armed Forces are also described. This publication can be found in many libraries and guidance offices, or may be purchased from the Superintendent of Documents, U.S. Government Printing Office, Washington, DC 20402.

H. TRAINING FOR AN ENVIRONMENTAL CAREER

Many postsecondary (after high school) educational institutions offer training programs concerned with environmental work. These schools— either traditional two-year or four-year colleges and universities or trade schools, technical institutes, vocational schools, or correspondence courses—are continually adding courses in environmental fields. After students have selected career fields and discussed them with counselors, parents, employment officers, persons established in careers, or other advisers, they should visit the school they are interested in attending and ask some some serious questions. Do students find jobs when they graduate? What specific courses are required, and what is the normal length of time for their completion? Who are the faculty? When you visit the school, talk with some of the students and find out what they think of the place. Also, while you are there, visit the financial aid office. If you cannot visit the school, write a personal letter with your questions. Perhaps, through the guidance office at your high school, you can find the name of a student at the school with whom you can correspond.

Students seeking undergraduate degrees should major in a traditional field rather than concentrate on environmental studies. Federal, state, and local government agencies often prefer to hire persons from traditional fields (such as chemistry, biology, or mathematics) and train them for environmental applications. Also, students with such educational backgrounds are in a strong position to compete for jobs in nonenvironmental areas if they are unable to find employment in environmental fields. You will always be able to specialize in an environmental field at the graduate level. Students selecting an undergraduate major should consider not only the degree of competition for environmental jobs, but also the possibility that they would want to change jobs in the future.

There are some environmental occupations, for example in the equipment operation and support groups, that are available for immediate entry with little or no previous training. For the most part, jobs in these areas are in local government systems under the public works department and are secured by contacting the city or county government personnel office (usually listed in the telephone directory).

Many state and local pollution control agencies conduct regular training programs for new-entry personnel who are beginning careers in environmental fields. Information regarding training may be obtained by contacting the appropriate state pollution control agency listed in the telephone directory.

Private industries and public utilities may send representatives to college campuses or to job fairs to recruit applicants for their businesses. You may also contact their personnel offices by telephone or letter. Often a resumé is helpful. This personal information sheet tells your future employer about your educational background, professional experience, and why you would like to work for their company.

Persons may get help from the local Job Service office of their state employment service. The state employment services are affiliated with the U.S. Employment Service of the U.S. Department of Labor's Employment and Training Administration. At each of the almost 2,500 Job Service offices located across the United States, jobseekers are helped in finding employment and employers are assisted in obtaining qualified workers.

I. WHAT HIGH SCHOOL COURSES ARE NEEDED FOR ENVIRONMENTAL CAREERS

In high school, prospective environmentalists should gain as broad a general background as possible. All of the environmental sciences and engineering careers require a basic understanding of biology, chemistry, and physics. If you intend to pursue an occupation that requires a minimum of a bachelor's degree, you should take a year's course in each of these three subjects. Students interested in technician-level careers should take biology and an applied science course, such as earth science.

Many students love biology in high school and hope to become ecologists; however, some shy away from taking physics or chemistry because they are afraid that the subjects might be too hard, or that they might require too much math ability, or for some other reason. Avoidance of these courses is very impractical for anyone interested in a career in environmental fields.

Physics is essential for environmentalists. It is the study of energy. Even wildlife biologists and oceanographers are deeply involved with physics in their work. How organisms obtain, store, and use energy is of vital importance in every branch of the life sciences. If you do not comprehend physics, you will not be able to explore the delicate energy transformations that take place between cell and sun, between cell and cell, and between the species of the earth. All of the life functions, such as digestion, circulation, and reproduction, involve physics, as well as the extra-organism studies such as ecology, evolution, animal behavior, and medical sciences. The oceans are vast storehouses of energy. Not only the mineral wealth at the sea bottom, but also the currents and waves contain an enormous fund of power that can be utilized.

Chemistry is the study of the components of matter. All living things, being forms of matter and composed of matter, are consequently made up of chemicals. There are thousands of unique chemicals within each living creature. They are in dynamic balance, and each chemical performs a special task. To understand the needs and functions of a flower, a fish, or any life form, the life scientist must know how the chemicals within each organism are formed and how they react.

Courses such as photography, art, drafting, and shop develop very special skills that can give you a special advantage in college, in applying for a job, and on the job. They are highly recommended.

Mathematics is the foundation of all the sciences. You should take four years of high school math. The scientific occupations require two years of algebra, one year of geometry, and one year of trigonometry. Precalculus, probability theory, statistics, and computer programming will be very helpful. A knowledge of computer programming and statistics is becoming essential for most advanced work. Business math will be very helpful for those who do not intend to pursue a four-year college program.

The need to communicate scientific ideas and discoveries requires good reading, writing, and speaking skills. You should have a good vocabulary and be able to express yourself clearly. High school English and speech courses will help you develop these abilities. Grammar, spelling, and vocabulary are just as important to a scientist as are knowing the parts of the body or knowing arithmetic. Failure to learn these subjects can be a constant embarrassment and can retard your future both in college and on the job. Mastering composition and studying great literature help to train your mind in logical thinking and sensitize your emotions to the feelings of society. With these skills you can analyze and organize your thoughts and your work, and you can carry out research that may be more responsive to the needs of mankind.

Twenty years ago, all physical scientists had to read German and usually one other foreign language in order to keep current in the research literature published in non-English journals. Today, it is not absolutely necessary to have a reading knowledge of foreign languages to suceed in the sciences, since translations of important publications are generally available. However, skill in understanding Russian, Chinese, French, or German is helpful to future environmentalists who want to communicate with their colleagues around the globe. Environmental problems are worldwide, and international cooperation will be required.

J. HOW YOU CAN FIND OUT MORE ABOUT ENVIRONMENTAL CAREERS

Your high school guidance counselor is one of your best sources for further information on selecting the right career. The counselor can talk with you realistically. He or she will have your grades, your teachers' recommendations, your aptitude test scores, and, perhaps, some kind of vocational or career survey that you have filled out. With that information and with your personal input, this professional can provide you with valuable insight and service. Many guidance departments keep files of job opportunities, college catalogs, and a reference library to help you.

There are many ways to find out more about careers in the environment. For information write to local, state, and Federal agencies and to special-interest national organizations. Watch for newspaper articles reporting current local efforts to deal with environmental problems. From these stories you may get ideas about future job needs in your community and can learn the names of people in charge of operations.

Probably the very best way to find out about any occupation is to interview people working in the field. Talk to someone mentioned in the newspaper report. Contact a local college or university and make an appointment to talk to a professor of engineering, chcmistry, or meteorology. Call up your local power company or the water treatment plant and ask if you can visit their facilities. If there is an energy company in your area, send them a note. Most people are happy to talk to students who are pursuing careers in their field.

Many schools have annual Career Nights, at which you have the opportunity to talk to people from many different occupations. Also your friends or relatives may know someone who works in a field closely related to your interests. The more people you see and the more information you have, the better chance you have of selecting a career that is right for you.

When you find someone, ask them: What's your job like? Tell me what you do in a typical day? What do you like best about your job? What do you like least? What made you decide to be an environmentalist? What are the prospects for employment in your field? What kind of training do you need? You can even ask them personal questions that might help to answer some of your concerns, such as: Suppose I am just pretty good in school. Will that affect my chances of entering your field? Can I be a mother and still work in your field? Do you ever do anything really exciting?

The following reference books may be helpful if you are still undecided as to which field would be best for you. Check at your school or town library for these and other publications.

Opportunities in Environmental Careers by Odum Fanning. A Vocational Guidance Manual available from Data Courier, Inc., 620 South 5th Street, Louisville, KY 40202. 1971 edition costs $3.95 (paper) plus 50¢ postage and handling. A good basic guide.

Career Opportunities: Ecology, Conservation and Environmental Control, published by J. G. Ferguson Publishing Co., Chicago, Illinois. 1971.

Careers for the '70's: Conservation by Ed Dodd, Crowell-Collier Press, New York, 1971.

Jobs That Save Our Environment by Melvin Berger, Lothrop, Lee & Shepard, New York, 1973, is good for elementary/jr. high students.

Conservation Directory (published annually) is available for $2.50 from the National Wildlife Federation, 1412 16th Street NW, Washington, DC 20036 and includes listings for government and state agencies, commissions, national and state private organizations, as well as colleges and universities that offer environmental studies programs. They also publish *Conservation Careers* (1975); single copies are free.

Chapter IV

"Pure Science" Careers That Aid the Environment

This chapter discusses what might be called "pure science" occupations involving the environment. Job descriptions are given for careers that require professional training in chemistry, physics, or biology. Information is presented on job opportunities and on educational requirements. The environmental careers discussed in detail are: water purification chemist, wastewater treatment chemist, air chemist, industrial waste chemist, agricultural chemist, toxicologist, solid state physicist, nuclear physicist, acoustical physicist, thermophysicist, agricultural service biologist, agronomist, entomologist, microbiologist, pathologist, environmental epidemiologist, fish biologist, wildlife biologist, ecologist, biochemist, food scientist, and biometrician. Over fifty other pure science environmental careers are also surveyed.

Scientists study the universe around us to learn why it behaves as it does. Scientists try to understand the living and physical world through observation, study, and experimentation. They investigate every aspect of our natural surroundings, from the center of the earth to the farthest star. They study things as small as the tiniest nuclear particle and as gigantic as a galaxy. Scientists examine bursts of energy lasting a millionth of a second as well as rock patterns formed over millions of years. Plants, animals, the oceans, the atmosphere all fall under the questioning eyes of scientists.

Many scientists are involved in work concerning the environment. Some, such as wastewater treatment chemists, work at examining the current conditions of the environment and developing methods for improving them. Others, such as plant physiologists, conduct research on improving organisms so that they can continue to flourish and even increase their yield in worsening conditions.

Jobs in the sciences can usually be divided into the physical sciences and the life sciences. Physical scientists represent the largest group. Most physical scientists are chemists.

Chemists study the 103 known elements. They examine how these

elements combine to form every substance in the universe, what properties they have, and how they react with each other. Chemists are able to
analyze a material to discover what substances were combined or mixed
together to compose it. A chemist can examine a sample of water and
determine which salts, minerals, and toxic substances are present.
Chemists can also synthesize new chemicals that can be useful as fertilizers, pesticides, fire retardants, and so on. Oil companies are hiring
chemists to find ways for changing coal, which is abundant in the United
States, to petroleum.

Physics is the other major branch of the physical sciences. Physics is
concerned with matter and energy. Physicists investigate the behavior of
light, heat, electricity, magnetism, gravity, and the properties of matter.
Environmental physicists are studying ways in which heat and energy
can be better utilized. Some are working on the development of solar
energy systems, while others are trying to improve the safety and efficiency of nuclear reactors. Physicists help provide new equipment and
techniques for solving such problems as automobile exhaust pollution,
excessive noise from aircraft and traffic, radiation control, and so on.

Life scientists investigate living things. Biological scientists, or
biologists, are concerned with how life began, how plants and animals
function, and how they can survive in our changing world. Biologists
usually specialize in a particular group of living things. Zoologists study
the animal kingdom, whereas botanists investigate the plant world.
Marine biologists examine the living world of the oceans, whereas microbiologists study bacteria, viruses, and countless other organisms that we
can see only with a microscope.

The discoveries of biologists are used by medical scientists to understand and control disease. Medical scientists differ from physicians.
Physicians, veterinarians, and dentists deliver health care, whereas
medical scientists do research in medical and health problems. Medical
scientists seek cures for diseases through research in laboratories,
whereas physicians work directly with sick people.

Preparation to become a scientist usually involves a minimum of a
bachelor's degree. Most jobs require a master's degree, and some a doctorate. Beginning scientists need a broad background in chemistry,
physics, and biology, as well as advanced training in mathematics and
computer science. They should have good laboratory skills.

It is highly recommended that an undergraduate student should not
specialize too early in his or her training. Graduate school provides the
opportunity for learning a specific branch of science, such as physiology,
toxicology, or synthetic chemistry. Most employers will train you for
their special interests, and they usually prefer a well-rounded employee

to an overspecialized one. Many scientists continue their education, and are able to upgrade their jobs, by going to graduate school part time, often at the expense and encouragement of their employer.

Scientists work in offices, laboratories, classrooms, and in the field. Some are exposed to health or safety hazards, but there is little risk if proper procedures are followed. Most scientists work regular hours. Except for agricultural and wildlife fields, most science jobs are in or near large metropolitan areas.

Let us look at the main branches of science and see the careers available in environmental specialties.

A. CHEMISTRY

Chemistry is the study of matter and how it changes. The chemist wants to know what substances are made of, how they react, and how they change. Chemists are curious about why rubber is soft and why a diamond is hard. Why does iron rust and silver tarnish, but gold stays shiny forever? Chemists have been responsible for the drugs that save lives, as well as for the pollutants that infect our environment. Chemistry is a tremendous industry, employing over half a million people and providing billions of dollars worth of consumer goods that have given our society its style, its comfort, its entertainment, and, regrettably, some of its problems.

Chemistry affects our lives in many ways. When you are sick, the physician prescribes a drug discovered and produced by chemists. Chemical research is responsible for synthetic fibers, plastics, and synthetic rubber used in the tires and other parts of automobiles. Synthetic fertilizers that increase the yield of food from each acre of land were developed in the laboratory. So were the insecticides that prevent the destruction of crops by insects.

The soap and toothpaste you use, as well as your toothbrush, hairbrush, and comb, are products from the chemical industry. Your perfume and your cologne are from the chemical cosmetic factories. If you look at the label on the side of a cereal box, you will discover a list of chemical additives including BHA or BHT, which were invented by chemists to keep the crackle in your puff.

Natural energy resources, such as gasoline, require complex chemical processes to change the thick crude oil into the clear, free-flowing liquid needed by an automobile engine. The car battery, too, is a product of a major branch of the chemical industry.

The production of many of these beneficial products, however, has also affected our environment in harmful ways. Poisonous wastes from a chemical plant in Japan found their way into fish living in the nearby waters. Many persons eating the fish died as a result of the poison. Industrial wastes buried near the Love Canal have risen to the surface, endangering the health of the community in New York State. The air around some manufacturing plants contains corrosive acid vapors as a result of industrial pollution. These can damage crops and wildlife and corrode buildings and monuments.

Manufacture of some products has created new and unexpected problems. Lead from the exhaust of automobiles released into the air has been carried all over the earth by currents in the atmosphere. It has even been found in ice at the North Pole. Similarly, fluorocarbons from spray cans are threatening the ultraviolet-light–absorbing ozone layer in the upper reaches of the stratosphere.

Even the manufacture of chemicals intended for beneficial purposes has not been without mishap. A drug called thalidomide, used by some pregnant women to help them sleep, resulted in deformities in their babies. The insecticide DDT nearly caused the extinction of several species of birds, including the bald eagle, our national symbol, before it was banned by law.

Chemists serve an important function in our society. They are well-paid, hard-working people who are trying to improve our lives. Now, through new laws and agencies such as the Environmental Protection Agency and the Federal Drug Administration, chemists are working with the government and with private citizen groups to protect our safety, our health, and our environment.

1. Environmental Chemistry Careers

Chemistry is divided into many branches that are not clearly distinguished. These branches developed as chemists began to specialize on various problems. There are five basic areas of chemistry: (1) organic chemistry, which is concerned with the chemical compounds that contain carbon; (2) inorganic chemistry, which is the study of the compounds of the other elements; (3) physical chemistry, which studies the physical characteristics of matter and seeks a mathematical explanation of chemical processes; (4) analytical chemistry, which is concerned with determining the composition of substances; and (5) biochemistry, which studies the chemical processes in living things.

A chemist normally receives a bachelor's degree that includes coursework in each of those five areas. Specialization usually occurs after the chemist finds a job or chooses a field for graduate study. Below are several jobs for chemists involving the environment. A student should not specifically prepare for any one of these careers until he or she has received the undergraduate degree.

An environmental chemist in the laboratory.

Water Purification Chemist

These chemists analyze water samples throughout the water treatment process. They test water samples for bacteria that are the key to health problems, for aesthetic quality or freedom from odor and taste, for turbidity or suspended solids, for chemical quality, and for other characteristics. They use highly sophisticated testing equipment such as infrared, ultraviolet, and visible spectrophotometers. They also test for pesticides and herbicides and the presence of radiation.

In addition to testing water samples, chemists determine the amounts of chlorine to be used to destroy the microbes and other harmful organisms. They determine the kind and amounts of other chemicals needed to remove minerals, acids, salts, and other organic and inorganic compounds from the water to clarify and soften it.

In analyzing and solving problems related to water purification, they frequently work with engineers, managers, biologists, other professionals, and citizen groups to find solutions to water treatment problems. Their work involves the application of the principles and techniques of analytical chemistry to determine the structure, composition, and nature of water. Analysis requires not only the subtle correlation of theory and experience but also a keen insight into the nature of interferences and problems associated with analyzing water.

Water purification chemists are employed in most large water treatment plants, which are usually located in the heavily populated areas. In smaller plants, the laboratory work may be done by an outside or a private laboratory.

Opportunities for chemists in water treatment plants are expected to increase as new plants are constructed to meet the needs of the expanding population. For public water systems to meet increased regulation and higher water quality standards, additional laboratory personnel will also be needed. Other water analysts are employed by private industry and by regulatory and government agencies.

Wastewater Treatment Chemist

The chemist in a wastewater treatment plant analyzes samples of streams, raw and treated wastewater, sludge, and other by-products of the wastewater treatment process to determine the efficiency of the plant processes and to insure that plant effluents meet local, state, and Federal requirements. The chemist decides what tests are needed and develops workable testing procedures to obtain the information in a minimum amount of time.

The chemist conducts highly specialized and complex chemical, bacteriological, and physical analyses of wastewater and samples. Some of these samples are taken within the plant before, during, and after treatment. These chemists test samples taken from major users of the treatment plant in order to monitor and regulate waste discharges into the sewer and treatment systems and to make surcharge assessments.

Often the sample or test solution is a complex mixture of many compounds and elements, and the identification of a specific element can require many hours of separation work to remove interfering constituents. These tests may involve many identification procedures and the use of sophisticated equipment.

Chemists may specialize in testing that requires special instruments such as the gas chromatograph, the atomic absorption spectrophotometer, or the infrared spectrophotometer. The chemists must be able to develop new techniques to use the equipment and also make adjustments and repairs on these complex electronic instruments.

Chemists take part in special research and studies on plant operations and the treatment unit processes. They often are asked to help identify problems in the wastewater treatment process and in developing new procedures with the most up-to-date equipment.

Federal legislation requires that local governments control water pollution and safeguard public health and welfare. It is anticipated that chemists will continue to be in demand to analyze wastewater samples and insure that the treatment processes and effluents meet current government requirements.

Air Chemist

Air chemists use their knowledge of chemical reactions to identify pollutants in the air and their effects on the environment. They utilize routine tests for common pollutants; but, when necessary, they also must develop more detailed analysis of substances filtered from air, smokestacks, or exhaust pipes.

To analyze a sample, the chemist uses a series of tests to determine what substances are in the sample and how much of each is present.

The pollutants in the air are not just dust, smoke, fumes, and normal gases, but also include substances created by the interaction of pollutants with moisture or sunlight forming acids or photochemical smog. The smog may be more dangerous than the original pollutants. Not all of the chemistry of smog and acid formation is fully understood, so some chemists are assigned to find out exactly what happens when various chemicals mix in the presence of moist air and sunshine.

Others investigate the effects of different pollutants on construction materials and on living tissue, using their knowledge of how chemicals interact. Still others develop simple, inexpensive tests that can be done routinely for common pollutants, study the effect of different pollutants on visibility, find out how pollution from supersonic airplanes is changing the earth's climate, or trace pollutants to the industrial plants from which they come.

Air chemists are employed by government agencies, by industries having air-pollution problems, by private consulting firms advising industries, and by colleges, universities, and nonprofit research organizations. Although there are job openings for chemists, there are not many opportunities to specialize in air quality. Most pollution-control chemists do not specialize in air, water, or soil, but analyze samples and work on pollution problems anywhere in the environment.

Industrial Waste Chemist

Industrial waste chemists are concerned with the treatment, storage, and disposal of industrial waste. This waste can be in air, in water, or in solid form (such as paper, metal, plastics, sludge, or any other materials that pose a pollution problem). Industrial waste chemists conduct chemical and physical tests on samples to evaluate the presence of toxic substances, unsuitable conditions in disposal systems, pollutants affecting water tables or rivers, and other conditions related to industrial waste.

These chemists spend much of their time in the laboratory. They calibrate, set up, maintain, and operate a variety of laboratory equipment. They perform many complex tests including chemical and physical analyses of water, sewage, industrial wastes, air, and other substances. They develop laboratory testing routines and decide on the most appropriate procedures, depending on the problem.

They conduct on-site investigations of disposal, treatment, and storage facilities. They examine abatement equipment, effluent content, hydrocarbon emissions, temperature conditions, retention time on water and air samples, and many other factors related to handling industrial waste. Their duties are somewhat similar to those of a chemist in a wastewater treatment plant, except that they are concerned with a wider range of pollution problems and have a somewhat broader scope of duties.

There should be a healthy labor market for the next few years for industrial waste chemists, partly because of the requirements of new Federal legislation concerning hazardous wastes and regulations on disposal practices.

Agricultural Chemist

Agricultural chemists work with farmers and agricultural biologists to improve crop yields and to protect the harvests from infestation. They may develop fertilizers and pesticides that not only aid production but are not harmful to the environment. They might make chemical analyses to determine the identity and concentration of substances that may be adulterants, contaminants, or potentially hazardous chemicals in agricultural products. Typical work includes consulting with farmers and assisting in the collection of samples. They may have to develop new methods for examining produce.

Agricultural chemists work closely with government agency personnel at Federal, state, and local levels, particularly in the enforcement of laws regulating to the inspection and manufacturing of agricultural products and chemicals. Some specialize in the quantitative (how much) and qualitative (what substance) analyses of certain materials, such as pesticides, fertilizers, spray residues, commercial cattle feeds and veterinary products, or work for specialized branches, such as the dairy industry, the poultry industry, orchards, or cereal growers.

Opportunities are projected to be very good for agricultural chemists. As the concern over health hazards and the need for greater yields on farm lands increase, there will be an increased need for their services. Even the growth of "organic farming" requires the services of these experts, since this new industry still uses weedkillers, fertilizers, and pesticides. The difference is that their chemicals are far safer, usually natural in origin, and often do not leave hazardous residues.

Toxicologist

While we have enjoyed the economic and social benefits of chemicals, we have not always realized the risks that may be associated with them. For many chemical substances, we have little knowledge of the ill effects they might cause after many years of exposure. The problem is compounded by a dramatic surge in the development of chemicals in the last thirty-five years; at this time at least a thousand new chemical substances are introduced each year. Much work must be done in toxicology to identify and evaluate the hazards that chemical substances and mixtures may pose to health and the environment.

Toxicologists may serve as research specialists or as staff advisers, depending on the work setting. In a public health or agricultural department career, toxicologists design and carry out studies to determine the physiological effects of various substances, chemicals, and products; and advise on the toxicological properties of chemicals in the event of health problems. They work with experimental study data, intepreting study and survey results as to toxicological properties and hazards. They also evaluate the adequacy of toxicological data gathered for review, and provide expertise in the evaluation of label claims prior to the registration of pesticides, chemicals, agricultural chemicals, and other products. In cases of accidental exposure or poisoning, they give advice as to the nature and degree of the toxic hazard involved, They also advise on precautionary labeling for the use of hazardous chemicals and products.

Many toxicologists are employed by chemical manufacturers in research and developmental work. They conduct extensive testing programs and devise testing procedures and standards that are followed in the required testing of chemicals for their effects on human health. Toxicologists must provide information and test data to the U.S. Environmental Protection Agency before the manufacture of a new chemical or before a new use is applied for an existing one. The new toxic substances legislation should contribute to the hiring of toxicologists. Opportunities in this field, especially for those with graduate training, should be good.

Other Chemical Occupations Associated with the Environment

Colloid chemistry is the study of materials such as emulsions, fogs, gels, and smokes. Colloid chemists are interested in improving aerosol sprays. They are also interested in filters that can separate pollutants from the air and from cigarette smoke. They work with photographic film developing, as well as in the milk industry.

Geochemistry is the study of substances in the earth and the chemical changes they undergo. Geochemists often analyze rock and land structures to determine if enough mineral or fuel deposits are present for profitable mining and drilling operations. Geochemists are working with oil companies today to find methods for extracting oil from shale rock and coal. Geochemists also work with archeologists and paleontologists to help us understand what life was like on earth hundreds, thousands, and millions of years ago.

Polymer chemists are interested in the long chain molecules that are useful in the home and in industry and are the essence of life. Polyethylene is the substance from which plastic bags are made. It is a polymer of ethylene, a light hydrocarbon obtained from the cracking of crude oil. It is relatively unreactive, so it can safely protect food. Other household polymers are teflon, vinyl, nylon, rayon, and dacron. Soap and detergents are polymers, as well as rubber and many pesticides. The long, spiral-staircase molecule DNA, which passes on genetic information from cell to cell, is a polymer, as are hemoglobin, insulin, and other proteins in the body.

Synthetic chemists try to put together simple compounds into complex materials that can be useful to industry and mankind. They make drugs, plastics, paints, food additives, lubricants, fibers, paper products, alloys, and on and on. They are the inventors in the field of chemistry. They decide what kind of physical and chemical properties a new substance must have to serve industry or a consumer need; then they set out to construct it in an inexpensive, productive way.

Radiochemists study chemical processes by using radioactive tracer materials. They have examined how drugs and chemicals work in the body, how sewage flows through waste disposal procedures, how oil flows through pipelines, and how oxygen is utilized in the photosynthetic reaction of plants. Rosalyn Yalow won the Nobel Prize for her work on how radioactive tracers can be used for diagnosing medical problems.

Analytical instrumentation chemists are used by industry, by research institutions, and by hospitals to identify and monitor chemical processes with the use of highly accurate instruments. Their instruments can often detect materials in the parts-per-billion range. They can identify what substance may be a causative agent in a disease or if a truly new material has been discovered. In the food industry, they continuously check batches of products for contamination and spoilage.

Pathological chemists study the chemical effects of disease on the body. They analyze diseased organs and tissues to determine how the chemical balance within the body was upset by the virus, the bacterium, the injury, or the cancer.

Metallurgical chemists are concerned with the manufacture of metals and their alloys. They try to develop combinations of metals with other compounds to produce materials with special properties. Anodized aluminum is light, colorful, rust-resistant, and strong. Titanium steel is so hard and strong that it is used in spacecraft designs.

Electrochemists study the generation of electricity in chemical reactions. The dry cell is an example of an electrochemical reaction. Special storage batteries are being developed that can hold the energy generated by solar batteries. Electrochemists are also concerned with corrosion, which involves the transfer of electrons, and with electroplating processes used in industry.

Nuclear chemistry involves the study of radioactive substances. During World War II nuclear chemists were stationed at Columbia University to develop chemical techniques for separating uranium-235, which is fissionable and can be used to make plutonium for an atomic bomb, from uranium-238. Glenn T. Seaborg received the Nobel Prize for heading the research teams that developed the transuranic elements, such as americium, einsteinium, californium, and berkelium.

Photochemists study the effect of light on substances. Photography is a chemical reaction that starts when light energy strikes the film. Photochemicals have been developed that can take pictures in virtual darkness, in outer space, and within living organisms. Sixty-second color developing is common. Photosynthesis is a photosynthetic reaction, and so is tanning. These, too, are being investigated by photochemists.

Radiation chemists study the chemical effects of chemical radiation on substances. Radiation can alter inorganic and biological chemical reactions. X-radiation, as well as light from laser radiation, is being used to monitor and control chemical reactions. The effect of low-energy radiation from such sources as microwave ovens is being studied by radiation chemists and medical personnel.

Structural chemists are interested in the ways in which atoms link to form molecules. They study crystals and try to develop new materials that have improved properties. One of the current branches of research in structural chemistry involves the production of microchips for computers. These ultrafine crystals have reduced the size of computers from giant room-size devices to calculators that can fit on the face of a watch dial.

Surface chemists study the chemical processes that take place at the surface of liquids and tiny solid particles. Detergents are the most common surface-active materials; however, surfactants are used in the oil and cosmetic industries and in many other fields. Surface chemists study the interfacial reactions that occur across cell membranes and are actively involved in studying reactions that occur when two media are in contact, such as in the production of nylon.

2. A Career as an Environmental Chemist

The need for environmental chemists came about as a result of environmental damage caused by pollutants. Most chemists working in the environmental field have degrees in one of the traditional branches of chemistry (organic, analytical, physical) and are considered environmental chemists because they work with data on the movement and fate of pollutants in the environment or work directly with environmental factors such as agriculture, water, petroleum, or geologic structures.

Chemists usually work in well-equipped laboratories. Often the work requires considerable standing. Chemists are expected to plan, organize, and carry out their assignments with a minimum of supervision. Problem-solving is an important part of this occupation. The chemist works with engineers and biologists to identify and solve present or potential problems. These could be wastewater treatment, toxic substances, air emissions, storage or disposal of industrial waste, or several problems combined.

The work requires the preparation of clear, scientifically sound, technically accurate, and informative reports. Communication skills are also needed to work with managers, professionals, and the public. In many laboratories, the chemist supervises assistants and possibly an aide.

A chemist should have an inquisitive mind, initiative, and the ability to work independently. Good eyesight and eye-hand coordination are also important for performing exact, detailed laboratory work.

Most chemists have baccalaureate degrees with major work in chemistry, biochemistry, or a closely related field. Some employers require two years of laboratory experience or an equivalent combination of experience and training. In some laboratories, additional coursework in instrumentation is needed to operate the specialized equipment. Research jobs in environmental chemistry usually require a master's degree or a doctorate.

In addition to the academic preparation, the chemist needs a thorough knowledge of the processes and industry in which he is employed and the pertinent local, state, and Federal requirements and regulations. This knowledge is usually obtained on the job.

Certification is not always required. However, some industrial chemists are encouraged to become certified, and it is usually a requirement for advancement.

Chemists with bachelor's degrees start at approximately $21,000, those with master's degrees at approximately $23,800, and those with doctorates at approximately $32,600. The average salary for a chemist in 1982 was $32,800.

3. *Where You Can Obtain Training in Chemistry*

Most universities and many four-year colleges offer baccalaureate degrees in chemistry. Some of these are:

University of Akron, Akron, Ohio 44325
University of Alaska, College, Alaska 99701
Antioch College, Yellow Springs, Ohio 45387
Barnard College, New York, N.Y. 10027
Bates Collge, Lewiston, Maine 04240
Baylor University, Waco, Texas 76703
Boston College, Chestnut Hill, Massachusetts 02167
Brown University, Providence, Rhode Island 02912
Bryn Mawr College, Bryn Mawr, Pennsylvania 19010
Carleton College, Northfield, Minnesota 55057
Carnegie-Mellon University, Pittsburgh, Pennsylvania 15213
The Citadel, Charleston, South Carolina 29409
Clemson University, Clemson, South Carolina 29631
Colby College, Waterville, Maine 04901
Colorado State University, Fort Collins, Colorado 80521
Cornell University, Ithaca, New York 14850
Davidson College, Davidson, North Carolina 28036
Delaware State College, Dover, Delaware 19901
Douglass College, New Brunswick, New Jersey 08102
Drake University, Madison, New Jersey 07940

Eastern Michigan University, Ypsilanti, Michigan 48197
Fairleigh Dickinson University, Rutherford, New Jersey 07070,
    and Teaneck, New Jersey 07666
Georgia Institute of Technology, Atlanta, Georgia 30332
Gettysburg College, Gettysburg, Pennsylvania 17325
Haverford College, Haverford, Pennsylvania 19041
Hiram College, Hiram, Ohio 44234
Howard University, Washington, D.C. 20001
Illinois Institute of Technology, Chicago, Illinois 60616
Knox College, Galesburg, Illinois 61401
La Salle College, Philadelphia, Pennsylvania 19141
Le Moyne College, Syracuse, New York 13214
Lebanon Valley College, Annville, Pennsylvania 17003
Loyola University, Chicago, Illinois 60611
Manhattan College, New York, N.Y. 10471
Marquette University, Milwaukee, Wisconsin 53233
Marshall University, Huntington, West Virginia 25705
McMurry College, Abilene, Texas 79605
Merrimack College, North Andover, Massachusetts 01845
University of Michigan, Ann Arbor, Michigan 48104
Middlebury College, Middlebury, Vermont 05753
University of Mississippi, University, Mississippi 38677
Monmouth College, Monmouth, Illinois 61462
Moravian College, Bethlehem, Pennsylvania 18018
Mount St. Vincent College, Riverdale, New York 10471
Muskingum College, New Concord, Ohio 43762
Nebraska Wesleyan University, Lincoln, Nebraska 68504
University of Nevada, Las Vegas, Nevada 89154
New York University, New York, N.Y. 10003
Norwich University, Northfield, Vermont 05663
Ohio State University, Columbus, Ohio 43212
University of Oregon, Eugene, Oregon 97403
Pacific Lutheran University, Tacoma, Washington 98447
Philadelphia College of Textiles and Sciences, Philadelphia,
    Pennsylvania 19104
University of Portland, Portland, Oregon 97203
Providence College, Providence, Rhode Island 02918
Reed College, Portland, Oregon 97202
Rice University, Houston, Texas 77001
Ripon College, Ripon, Wisconsin 54971
University of Rochester, Rochester, New York 14627
Sam Houston State University, Huntsville, Texas 77340
Simmons College, Boston, Massachusetts 02115

University of South Carolina, Columbia, South Carolina 29208
University of South Florida, Tampa, Florida 33620
St. John Fisher College, Rochester, New York 14618
St. Lawrence University, Canton, New York 13617
St. Louis University, St. Louis, Missouri 63103
State University of New York (Albany, Binghamton, Buffalo,
    Stony Brook, Cortland, Fredonia, Geneseo, New Paltz, Oneonta,
    Oswego)
Stetson University, Deland, Florida 32720
Swarthmore College, Swarthmore, Pennsylvania 19081
Syracuse University, Syracuse, New York 13210
Texas Christian University, Forth Worth, Texas 76129
Trinity University, San Antonio, Texas 78284
Tufts University, Medford, Massachusetts 02155
Tulane University, New Orleans, Louisiana 70118
University of Tulsa, Tulsa, Oklahoma 74104
Vanderbilt University, Nashville, Tennessee 37240
Vassar College, Poughkeepsie, New York 12601
University of Virginia, Charlottesville, Virginia 22903
Wake Forest University, Winston-Salem, North Carolina 27109
Washington and Jefferson College, Washington, Pennsylvania 15301
Wellesley College, Wellesley, Massachusetts 02181
Wesleyan College, Middletown, Connecticut 06457
Westminster College, Fulton, Missouri 65251
Widener College, Chester, Pennsylvania 19013
College of William and Mary, Williamsburg, Virginia 23185
Williams College, Williamstown, Massachusetts 01267
College of Wooster, Wooster, Ohio 44691
Yale College, New Haven, Connecticut 06520

4. More Information on Chemistry Careers

To obtain more information on careers in chemistry, write to:

American Chemical Society
1155 16th Street, NW
Washington, DC 20036

Manufacturing Chemists Association
1825 Connecticut Avenue, NW
Washington, DC 20009

The American Institute of Chemical Engineers
345 East 47th Street
New York, NY 10017

For information concerning Federal employment write to:

Interagency Board of U.S. Civil Service Examiners for
    Washington, DC
1900 E Street, NW
Washington, DC 20415

You may want to read:
Exploring Careers in Science by Stanley Jay Shapiro.
Richards Rosen Press, Inc.

B. PHYSICS

Physics is the science concerned with the properties of matter and the laws that describe how energy and matter behave. Through systematic observation and experimentation, physicists describe in mathematical terms the structure of the universe and the ways in which energy and matter interact. Physicists develop theories that describe the fundamental forces and the laws of nature. Determining the basic laws governing phenomena such as gravity, electromagnetism, and nuclear interaction leads to discoveries and innovations. For instance, the development of irradiation therapy equipment that destroys harmful growths in humans without damaging other tissues resulted from research in nuclear radiation. Physicists have contributed to scientific progress in areas such as nuclear energy, electronics, communications, aerospace, and medical instrumentation.

1. Environmental Physics Careers

A person who is interested in environmental problems and who enjoys physics and mathematics may be able to pursue a career in which research in physics is applied to environmental concerns. However, there are no actual careers for which you can apply or receive specific training under the title Environmental Physics. A physicist normally receives a bachelor's degree in physics, for which he or she has studied mechanics, electricity, magnetism, optics, thermodynamics, atomic and molecular physics, chemistry, and advanced mathematics. Then the student has to attend graduate school. A master's degree or a doctorate is required for most work in physics. At graduate school, the student receives advanced training in a specialized branch of physics. There are many specialties in physics that are involved in environmental work, and these are described below.

3M PHOTO

Environmental scientists prepare to analyze a wastewater sample by a powerful new analytical tool, high performance liquid chromatography (HPLC).

Solid State Physicist

These physicists investigate the properties of materials such as metals, alloys, semiconductors, and insulators. They supply information that can be applied to development of better energy utilization and production. Solid state physicists study the physical properties and atomic structures of solids, particularly crystals. Their work has already led to the development of the computer and the solar battery. Current research involves improvement of the storage battery, development of the catalytic converters used to retard air pollution, development of synthetic fuels, and other basic areas of environmental research.

Nuclear Physicist

These physicists are interested in the central core of the atom. They use large particle accelerators to smash nuclei in order to discover what they are made of and how they are held together. Nuclear energy is used for defense and in medical research. Nuclear power has a wonderful potential for solving many of the world's energy needs, but it must be properly controlled to protect the environment.

Nuclear physicists are working with engineers at developing safer nuclear power plants. They are also trying to find risk-free ways of storing radioactive wastes.

Some physicists specialize in radiation safety. These radiation protection specialists inspect X-ray equipment and radiation therapy machines to make sure that they are not hazardous to users. They conduct research on radiation exposure limits and safe work methods with radiation-producing devices, and they develop decontamination procedures. Some radiation physicists conduct training sessions and teach monitoring procedures concerning radiation hazards to technicians working with dangerous radiation equipment.

Acoustical Physicist

These scientists study sound and its transmission. Among their interests is noise pollution, and many work as consultants to manufacturers, engineering firms, builders, and city planners to prevent excess noise from occurring or to help muffle sounds that are damaging the environment. Many acoustical physicists work in the field of transportation, where they study ways to eliminate or control shock or vibration. Some work on quieting highway and air traffic noise by the use of special sound-absorbing barriers. Some may work with physicians and medical researchers in the study of the physiology and psychology of noise so that more efficient methods for noise control can be established.

Thermophysicist

Thermophysicists study how heat can be changed into work, how it is produced, how it is transferred from one place to another, and how it changes matter. Heat energy pushes the pistons of engines and turns the blades of turbines. It can easily be turned into electrical or mechanical energy. Over one-third of the fuel in today's automobile engines is wasted as heat energy instead of being efficiently converted to mechanical power. Thermophysicists are looking for ways to produce engines that will run cooler and provide more horsepower for the fuel they burn. The microwave oven is a new tool invented by physicists that flip-flops the molecules in foods, cooking them faster and with less energy than with ordinary electric stoves.

Electricity and magnestism are closely related. Electricity can produce magnetism, and magnetism can produce electricity. Physicists who unraveled this important relationship led man to the modern age. Huge generators provide the electric current that runs the labor-saving devices in our homes and the powerful machines in industry. Electricity provides light, heat, and air conditioning. Physicists are constantly working at improvements and innovations in the field of electromagnetism.

2. *A Career as an Environmental Physicist*

Environmental physicists apply their training as scientists to solve problems involving the physical, natural, and social world. They use their expertise to help other environmentalists. They may be involved in preparing environmental impact statements with city planning agencies, or working with lawyers and politicians in writing regulations for radiation control. They may investigate hazards, prepare evidence, and testify in court. They might work with engineers and chemists in designing fuel-efficient engines and turbines and systems for turning coal into petroleum or solar energy into electricity. They may write technical reports and educational materials as well as deliver talks on the health effects of noise or radiation. A few environmental physicists may concentrate on one area of interest, but usually environmental issues are combined with other concerns.

Graduate training in physics or a closely related field is almost essential for most entry-level jobs in physics and for advancement in all types of work. The doctorate usually is required for full faculty status at colleges and universities and for industrial or government jobs administering research and development programs.

University programs specifically designed for a career in environmental physics are lacking; however, training in the following courses will help you: engineering, acoustics, computer science, environmental planning, environmental or public health, and the basics of management. Courses in writing, speech, and psychology provide preparation for presenting information convincingly. Work experience is a valuable asset to your training.

Most careers have on-the-job training where the environmental physicist learns regulations and the principles, practices, and policies of the employing company or agency.

Students planning a career in physics should have an inquisitive mind, high mathematical ability, and imagination. They should be able to work on their own, since physicists, particularly in basic research, often receive only limited supervision. And they should be able to work as part of a research team with scientists from other disciplines.

Physicists often begin their careers doing routine laboratory tasks. After some experience, they are assigned more complex tasks and may advance to work as project leaders or research directors. Some advance to top management jobs where they direct government research agencies or multinational corporations. Physicists who develop new products frequently form their own companies or join new firms to exploit their original ideas.

It is anticipated that a growing interest in environmental control will result in increased employment of environmental physicists. At present there is a shortage, but openings are limited by a lack of funds. Opportunities are best for those who have advanced degrees and are willing to live wherever the jobs are available.

Inexperienced physicists with bachelor's degrees start at approximately $22,000, those with master's degrees at approximately $26,500, and those with doctorates at approximately $34,000. The average salary for a physicist in 1982 was $33,000.

3. Where You Can Obtain Training in Physics

Most universities and many four-year colleges offer baccalaureate degrees in physics. Some of these are:

Adelphi University, Garden City, New York 11530
University of Arizona, Tucson, Arizona 85721
Brooklyn College, Brooklyn, New York 11210
Bucknell University, Lewisburg, Pennsylvania 17837
California Institute of Technology, Pasadena, California 91109
University of California, Berkeley, California 94720, Los Angeles, California 90024, Santa Barbara, California 93106
California State University, Fullerton, California 92634
Case Western Reserve University, Cleveland, Ohio 44106
University of Colorado, Boulder, Colorado 80302
Cooper Union, New York, N.Y. 10003
Cornell University, Ithaca, New York 14850
Drexel University, Philadelphia, Pennsylvania 19104
Fairleigh Dickinson University, Rutherford, New Jersey 07070
Georgia Institute of Technology, Atlanta, Georgia 30332
Harvard University, Cambridge, Massachusetts 02138
Harvey Mudd College, Claremont, California 91711
University of Illinois, Urbana, Illinois 61801
Iowa State University, Ames, Iowa 50010
Louisiana State University, Baton Rouge, Louisiana 70803
Manhattan College, New York, N.Y. 10471
University of Maryland, College Park, Maryland 20742

Massachusetts Institute of Technology, Cambridge,
  Massachusetts 02139
Miami University, Oxford, Ohio 45056
University of Michigan, Ann Arbor, Michigan 48104
Michigan State University, East Lansing, Michigan 48824
University of Minnesota, Minneapolis, Minnesota 55455
New Mexico State University, Las Cruces, New Mexico 88003
New York University, New York, N.Y. 1003
Oberlin College, Oberlin, Ohio 44074
Ohio State University, Columbus, Ohio 43212
Pennsylvania State University, University Park, Pennsylvania 16802
Purdue University, West Lafayette, Indiana 47907
Rensselaer Polytechnic Institute, Troy, New York 12181
Rice University, Houston, Texas 77001
Rutgers University, New Brunswick, New Jersey 08903
State University of New York, Stony Brook, New York 11790
Tufts University, Medford, Massachusetts 02155
U.S. Air Force Academy, U.S.A.F.A, Colorado 80840
U.S. Naval Academy, Annapolis, Maryland 21402
Virginia Polytechnical Institute, Blacksburg, Virginia 24061
University of Wisconsin, Madison, Wisconsin 53706
Yale University, New Haven, Connecticut 06520

4. More Information on Physics Careers

The American Institute of Physics has a number of member societies that can help you in selecting a career.

The American Physical Society has as its objective the advancement and diffusion of the knowledge of physics. All branches of fundamental and applied physics are generally included in its scope. Both experimental and theoretical researches are reported in its journals and meetings.

The Optical Society of America devotes itself to the advancement of optics, pure and applied, in all its branches. Its scope includes research in fundamental optics as well as problems concerned with design and production of optical instruments.

The Acoustical Society of America has as its purpose to increase and diffuse the knowledge of acoustics and promote its practical applications. The scope includes architectural acoustics, engineering acoustics, noise, psychological and physiological acoustics, shock and vibration, speech communication, underwater acoustics, physical acoustics, and musical acoustics.

The Society of Rheology is composed of physicists, chemists, and engineers interested in rheology, which is defined as the science of deformation and flow of matter. Rheology includes both phenomenological and molecular theories, instrumentation, and the study of materials such as plastics, metals, ceramics, rubbers, paint, glass, and foodstuffs.

The American Association of Physics Teachers provides a much needed forum for the discussion of the problems of teaching. In cooperation with other groups, it promotes the advancement of physics and emphasizes its place in the general culture.

The American Crystallographic Association has as its objective the promotion of the study of the arrangement of the atoms in matter, its causes, its nature, and its consequences, and of the tools and methods used in such studies.

The American Astronomical Society has as its purpose the advancement of astronomy and closely related branches of science.

The American Association of Physicists in Medicine has as its purposes to promote the application of physics to medicine and biology, to encourage interest and training in medical physics and related fields, and to disseminate technical information in medical physics.

The American Vacuum Society has as its purpose the advancement and diffusion of the knowledge of vacuum science, both fundamental and applied. Its scope includes all areas of science and technology wherein pressures below atmospheric are essential.

Write to them at:

The American Institute of Physics
335 East 45th Street
New York, NY 10017

They also have a student program, called the Society of Physics Students, which you may be interested in joining.

For more information concerning Federal employment write to:

Interagency Board of U.S. Civil Service
1900 E Street, NW
Washington, DC 20415

For detailed information about careers in physics, read:

Your Future in Physics by Raymond M. Bell.
　　Richards Rosen Press, Inc.
Your Future in Nuclear Energy Fields, by W. E. Thomson.
　　Richards Rosen Press, Inc.

Exploring Careers in Science, by Stanley Jay Shapiro.
Richards Rosen Press, Inc.

C. LIFE SCIENCES

Life scientists study the nature, structure, function, and behavior of living things. They are concerned not only with the myriad forms of life but also with evolution, the physical, social, and psychological development of organisms, and the relationships between living things and the environment. Biology is too broad a science for any single person to comprehend or to investigate; therefore, life scientists specialize in one of the many branches of the science.

All of the fields of the life sciences, however, are related to each other in some way. Even the traditional delineations of botany and zoology cannot stay distinct, since a scientist studying even one specific organism must encompass in his or her research the habitat, evolution, structure, chemistry, weather conditions, predators, food, and so forth with which the life form coexists.

All life scientists are environmentalists. Their work must emphasize the relationship of animals and plants to their environment. Many conduct basic research to increase our knowledge of living organisms that can be applied in medicine, in increasing crop yields, and in improving wildlife. When working in laboratories, life scientists must be familiar with research techniques and laboratory equipment such as the electron microscope. Knowledge of computers also is useful in conducting experiments. Not all research, however, is performed in laboratories. Field study is an important tool for the environmental life scientist. A wildlife scientist may live among a pride of lions in Africa in order to understand their behavior in nature, or a botanist may explore a volcanic Alaskan valley to investigate what plants grow there.

About one-fifth of all life scientists work in management or administration, ranging from planning and administering programs for testing foods and drugs to directing activities at zoos or botanical gardens. Some life scientists work as consultants to business firms or to the government. Many teach at universities or colleges, where they carry out research projects while training undergraduate and graduate students.

1. Environmental Life Science Careers

Some of the life science careers that are directly involved in dealing with the environment are:

Agricultural Services Biologist

Agricultural services biologists are concerned with assuring the exclusion of pests and with the raising of both agricultural and ornamental plants. Increasingly, emphasis in pest control is on using biological rather than chemical means of eradication. In biological control natural forces and predators are used to eliminate pests, instead of harmful chemicals.

Agricultural biologists study the insects, weeds, rodents, fungi, bacteria, and viruses that destroy crops. They learn the life cycles of the pests, the hosts that carry them, the conditions needed for them to thrive, and the situations that destroy them. If the biologists can discover a natural way of eliminating a pest, that method can be introduced to farmers.

These biologists may work in any number of environmental settings. Those engaged in research may work as members of technical staffs, conducting pesticide use analysis and development research both on chemical and biological methods. As long as chemical control methods are being used, agricultural biologists must work with chemists to develop new and safer substances. Pests also become resistant to chemicals relatively quickly.

Agricultural services biologists may specialize in plant nursery and seed fields, where they do research in developing hybrid plants that are disease- or pest-resistant. Some specialize in plant diseases, weed pest problems, insects, or special kinds of crops. Others assist in the development of inspection techniques and serve as advisers on regulations concerning exportation and importation of agricultural commodities from other countries, states, or counties.

Agronomist

These life scientists work with farmers. They are concerned with developing and improving the quality of crops, such as corn, wheat, and cotton. They try to find better ways for planting, growing, and harvesting grains, fruits, and vegetables. They work with agricultural chemists to produce fertilizers. Often, through research with geneticists, new breeds of crops can be developed that are healthier and more resistant to disease and insect infestation. New crops can also be designed to grow faster or with special properties that will make them more desirable to farmers, wholesalers, and consumers.

Other Agricultural Scientists

Plant anatomists are interested in the structural parts of plants. They are concerned with the roots, the stems, and the leaves. Botanists want to know how the plant makes its food. Plant biochemists study the photosynthetic reaction. Others are interested in the nongreen plants, which cannot directly convert sunlight into food.

There are life scientists who want to discover the mechanisms by which water and minerals are circulated throughout the plant. Plant geneticists are studying the ways in which plants reproduce. They want to know the interrelationships between the fruit, the seed, and the flower. They strive to make sturdier, healthier plants.

Plant pathologists (phytopathologists) study diseases in plants and work with plant physiologists and biochemists in developing cures. Crop production is also dependent on an understanding of the soil, so agronomists work with soil scientists to determine ways of increasing acreage yields and decreasing soil erosion.

Horticulturists work with orchard and garden plants such as fruit and nut trees, vegetables, and flowers. They try to improve the various varieties. Horticulturists are involved in the beautification of communities, homes, parks, and other areas as well as increasing crop quality and yields.

Entomologist

Entomology is the science that deals with insects. Because there are so many insect species, and because they are of such great economic importance to the agricultural industry, there are biologists who have divided the field into two specialties: systematic entomology and economic entomology.

The systematic entomologist is a laboratory and research worker concerned with the identification and classification of insects, whereas the economic entomologist works directly with control of insect pests. Some researchers study mosquito control, plant protection, pest control management, or pesticide cost benefits.

Economic entomologists conduct control and eradication projects or aid cities and counties in detection surveys. Surveys are conducted to determine the extent and status of insects pests (such as the Mediterranean fruit fly, or medfly) and their economic impact on hosts (such as citrus crops) and to propose a repertoire of intense control procedures. In the course of this work they secure bids from commercial pest control operators and formulate contracts for the application of insecticides or other procedures. Also, they evaluate the effectiveness of procedures used for surveying and pest control.

Systematic entomologists work primarily in laboratories, where they prepare and identify native and foreign insects and compile data on the distribution and status of insects of economic significance. They collect research information relative to injurious insects and maintain properly classified reference collections of insects.

Microbiologist

Bacteriological testing is the key to health protection. Microbiologists, or bacteriologists, take bacteria counts on water samples, sludges, and sewage in controlling pollution. They isolate and make laboratory cultures of significant bacteria and other microorganisms from samples and then examine them through a high-powered microscope. These microorganisms can be harmful and must be identified in order to protect citizens who drink the water, breath the air, swim in the pond, eat the food, and so forth.

EXXON PHOTO

A microbiologist prepares plants for bacteriologic samples.

Microbiologists maintain precise records of test results. They prepare reports and other studies concerning the quality of treated water, wastes, and foods. They work with chemists, engineers, and treatment plant personnel in controlling the health safety of the environment.

Microbiologists work in water and wastewater treatment plants, health departments, hospitals, medical laboratories, and regulatory agencies. Some are engaged in research or teaching at a university or in private industry.

Pathologist

Working along with microbiologists, the pathologists specialize in disease. They study the effects of diseases, parasites, and insects on human and animal cells, tissues, and organs. Plant pathologists, sometimes called phytopathologists, are interested in the various bacteriological and viral infections that affect plants.

The information derived from the research laboratory of the pathologist is used by other biologists either in preventing the disease by eliminating the organism that causes the infection or in developing treatment procedures to help the affected plant, animal, or person.

Pathologists work for state or Federal departments of agriculture, public health departments, universities, hospitals, and private medical and research laboratories.

Environmental Epidemiologist

Epidemiology is concerned with diseases that infect large numbers of people. Public health epidemiologists may investigate widespread diseases such as Hong Kong flu or smallpox. Environmental epidemiologists conduct research on the distribution of diseases in industrial environments, and in their effect on groups of people rather than on a single individual. The work is also concerned with the health effects of selected chemicals and radiation.

These biologists rely heavily on statistical analyses and use the computer extensively. They compare the mortality (death rates) and morbidity (disease rates) of selected working populations against standard normal populations. If, for instance, five out of one hundred workers at the XYZ Chemical Company develop lung cancer after twenty years' exposure as compared to five out of one thousand workers in the normal population, there is strong evidence that the working conditions at the company severely endanger the employees.

In experimental epidemiology, the scientist may produce epidemics in laboratory animals for the study of certain problems. Some epidemiologists must negotiate with representatives of industry to select occupational groups for study, maintain contact with personnel of government agencies to obtain research data, and coordinate data collection and evaluation work.

Opportunities are very good in both private industry and government. However, most epidemiologists have an MD, a PhD, or both.

Fish Biologist

Fish biologists promote the growth and reproduction of fish in nature and in hatcheries. At one time, the main activity of the fish biologist was the restocking of lakes and streams. Now, it is improving and protecting habitats so that fish have a place to thrive. The fish biologist samples and tests water, looking for sources of pollution and for sites where fish can safely live and grow. To study a lake, the biologist collects samples of the fish population. From the samples, using statistical methods, the biologist is able to estimate how many fish are in the lake or region and prepare growth curves for the various species collected. Sample fish are dissected, the stomach contents analyzed, and any parasites present identified. The biologist collects samples, too, of aquatic insects and other organisms that fish eat. Using all the information gathered, the biologist makes recommendations as to how many and what kinds of fish might be added to the lake and how much fishing can be permitted.

The fish biologist assists in preparing environmental impact statements, predicting what effect a power dam, highway, or irrigation project will have on fish populations and suggesting ways to prevent fish loss.

If excessive dead fish are discovered, the biologist investigates the cause, such as silt, oil spill, industrial waste, or disease. Hundreds of thousands, even millions of fish sometimes die at one time. When those responsible can be identified, the biologist may testify in court to settle claims or to prosecute polluters.

Some fish biologists study the life span and migration of fish, determine what pollutants are harmful and in what amounts, or develop new diets, vaccines, and methods of crossbreeding. Some plan and direct hatchery operations for the state and Federal governments.

Usually a fish biologist specializes in freshwater fish or in marine (saltwater) fish. Although fish farming is a growing industry, the competition for jobs as fish biologists is very high. Each year more students graduate with degrees in fish biology than there are career openings.

Wildlife Biologist

The wildlife biologist defends our natural heritage of birds and other wildlife by studying their habits and the conditions they need for survival and by educating people on how to save wildlife.

Wildlife biologists count animals and study their distribution and migration, often observing them from an airplane or tracking them by radio. They study interrelationships between different kinds of animals and attempt to find a balance so that there are not more animals than food. They study the effects of pollutants, such as mercury and pesticides, on wildlife; plan sanctuaries to safeguard threatened animals; and artificially raise rare animals, such as whooping cranes, to prevent their extinction. They use statistical methods in analyzing animal populations and complex mathematical formulas for computer analysis of possible methods for reclaiming polluted land. They often act as consultants to foresters and range managers who oversee and develop wilderness areas.

Machines change animal environments. An increase in water temperature or the rerouting of a stream, the clearing of a forest, the draining of a swamp, the overgrazing of land, or the building of a city are events that have immediate effects on wildlife. Wildlife biologists prepare environmental impact statements, predicting what effect large development programs will have on the environment. Environmental impact statements have resulted in the redesign of plans for some projects.

Wildlife biologists also prepare educational materials, such as checklists of the birds and animals a visitor may find in a particular park, displays for nature centers, television news stories, and wildlife films. Some specialize in writing or in photography.

Openings are few for wildlife biologists. This is a competitive field with more qualified graduates than jobs. Some wildlife biologists must go into related occupations, such as biological laboratory work, teaching, or managing specialized farm lands.

Ecologist

Ecologists study the relationship between organisms and their environments. They investigate how such environmental influences as rainfall, temperature, pollutants, and other forms of animal and plant life affect organisms. Ecologists may examine samples of plankton, microscopic plants and animals, from the sea to determine the effects on ocean life of oil spills from tankers. They may go to the tops of mountains to count eagle chicks whose shells were affected by DDT. Some urban ecologists constantly monitor the water and air in our cities for various pollutants.

Other Biology Fields Directly Involving the Environment

Biosociologists study how groups of living things get along together. They are interested in schools of fish, gaggles of geese, herds of elephants, and so forth. They are also interested in the interrelationships between several species that might share a meadow or a watering hole.

Biogeographers study the geographical distribution of living things. Similar plants and animals in Africa and South America suggest that once a giant continent separated, splitting into our modern land forms. Phytogeographers specialize in plants and the land forms where they exist, and zoogeographers specialize in animal forms at different geologic locations.

Biological limnologists study living things in rivers and lakes. Marine biologists are concerned with living species in the oceans. Biometeorologists are concerned with those in the atmosphere, such as airborne bacteria. And exobiologists study living things in space and on other planets.

Zoologists study various aspects of animal life—its origins, behavior, and life processes. Some zoologists study live animals in laboratory, zoological park, or natural surroundings. Others dissect animals to study the structure of their parts.

Many fields of zoology are identified by the animal groups studied. Mammalogists study mammals, ornithologists study birds, herpetologists study reptiles and amphibians, ichthyologists are interested in fish, entomologists study insects, helminthologists study worms, and protozoologists investigate the lives and behavior of one-celled animals.

Animal husbandry specialists do research on the breeding, feeding, and diseases of farm animals. Veterinarians study diseases in animals and learn to treat their ailments and complaints.

Biochemist

Biochemistry involves the use of chemistry in the study of living things. Biochemists study the chemical composition and behavior of organisms. Life is, simply, a product of complex chemical combinations and reactions. Therefore, to understand how nature works, biochemists investigate the chemistry of reproduction, growth, heredity, respiration, and so on.

Photosynthesis, for example, is the chemical combination of water and carbon dioxide, in the presence of light, to make sugar. The reactants and the products have been known for over two hundred years; however, the mechanism, or means, by which the reaction takes place is still not completely understood. There is now strong evidence to suggest that the light reaction of photosynthesis involves two simultaneous systems. One involves chlorophyll a-type molecules and a very strong electron acceptor, called ferredoxin, which passes the energy to nicotine amide dinucleotide phosphate. The second stage involves chlorophyll b-type molecules, carotenes, and plastoquinones. As you can see, biochemistry is far more complicated than the simplistic reactions outlined in your high school textbooks.

The methods and techniques of biochemistry are applied in medicine, nutrition, and agriculture. Biochemists may investigate the causes and cures for diseases, identify the nutrients necessary to maintain good health, or develop chemical compounds for pest control.

Some specialties related closely to biochemistry are nutrition and pharmacology. Nutritionists examine the bodily processes through which food is utilized and transformed into energy. They learn how vitamins, minerals, proteins, and other nutrients build and repair tissues. They are concerned with developing diets for ill patients, as well as advising healthy people on what to eat in order to maintain their well-being.

Pharmacologists develop and test new drugs. They use animals such as rats, guinea pigs, and monkeys to determine the effects of new products.

Long before a drug is marketed, the pharmacologist must prove that it is not harmful and that it is effective in treating the disorder. They also test the effects of gases, poisons, pollutants, cigarettes, and other substances on the functioning of organs and tissues.

Food Scientist

In the past, most food preparation was carried out in the home. People would either eat freshly prepared produce or store it in cellars. The stored foods were pickled, smoked, or salted. Today, however, almost all foods are processed in industry. A key worker involved in seeing that you have safe foods is the food scientist or food technologist. Food scientists apply their knowledge of chemistry, biology, and physics to the processing, preserving, packaging, distributing, and storing of food. About three-fifths of all food scientists work in developing new techniques for handling food. They research new sources for protein; examine the factors that affect the flavor, texture, or appearance of foods; and study the effects of microorganisms in the decay of products. Many food technologists work in quality assurance laboratories, periodically examining and inspecting food products.

Biometrician

Biometricians or biostatisticians advise environmental scientists and others on the use of statistical methods, both in planning research and in interpreting the results.

How can one be sure that a sample of air or of fish from a lake, for example, is representative? How much error can be expected in a study? These are some of the questions biometricians answer for research workers.

For example, one biometrician is helping an air scientist compare figures on the number and severity of brown lung disease cases with the amount of cotton dust found in the workers' factory. Another is helping to interpret experiments on mouse embryos to determine what pollutants cause birth defects. An industrial hygienist has discovered that employees of one factory have a higher rate of cancer than is found in the general population; a biometrician will help decide whether the higher rate is significant or due to chance.

Biometricians must be good biologists and have advanced training in mathematics, computer science, and statistics. They are needed wherever there is research. Public concern about the environment and the development of science determines how much research is done, but the need for biostatisticians is greater than the supply.

2. A Career as an Environmental Biologist

There were about 225,000 persons working as life scientists in 1978. About one-third are involved in work dealing with food and agriculture, about one-half work as biologists, and the rest are involved in biochemistry and medical science research.

Colleges and universities employ nearly three-fifths of all life scientists, in both teaching and research jobs. Medical schools and hospitals employ large numbers of life scientists.

Sizeable numbers of biologists work for state agricultural departments, which are usually associated with colleges and agricultural experiment stations. At these bureaus, agronomists improve crops, horticulturalists develop techniques for growing fruits and new species of flowers, veterinary scientists work on cures for animal diseases, entomologists study how bees cultivate orchards, and much vital farm research is carried out.

Food scientists in Idaho work with potato growers, as well as with frozen food processors and potato chip manufacturers. In Michigan they work with cereal manufacturers. Food chemists have found ways of rapidly ripening tomatoes so that they can be picked prematurely in Florida and under their supervision sprayed with ethylene glycol before being shipped North.

About 30,000 life scientists worked for the Federal government in 1978. Over half worked for the Department of Agriculture, which has research and aide stations throughout the U.S. A large agricultural station is in Beltsville, Maryland, where turkeys have been bred with overdeveloped breasts, since most Americans prefer white meat. Large numbers of life scientists work for the Department of the Interior and in the National Institutes of Health. One group at the Department of the Treasury examines alcohol and cigarette products for taxation violations. Another team at the Department of Commerce checks fibers for the textile industry. At the National Institutes of Health, government-financed disease research is being carried out by the leading life scientists of our country. At this huge research facility, in Bethesda, Maryland, intensive studies are being carried out on cancer, heart disease, mental disorders, birth defects, and many other serious ailments that require expensive, intensive research.

State and local governments employed about 30,000 life scientists. In addition to those working on agricultural products, many work for public health departments and environmental protection agencies, where they inspect restaurants and groceries, food-processing plants, and water and sewage facilities and check the air, the rivers, and so on. Nutritionists work for schools and hospitals, insuring that proper foods are served.

Approximately 50,000 life scientists worked in private industry. Most of them worked for companies that manufactured drugs, insecticides, or cosmetics, or they worked in the food industry. Some develop products in a research laboratory, and others do quality checks off an assembly line.

Biological laboratory research involves weighing, filtering, distilling, drying, and culturing (growing microorganisms). Precision and patience are of the utmost importance in laboratory science. Biological research often calls for working with animals. Sometimes the animal must be sacrificed, and often it is subjected to harsh treatment so that we can learn about nature and find ways to help humans suffering from terrible diseases. No biologist should be too squeamish about blood or about dissecting animals; that is how science progresses.

Biologists use a variety of tools and instruments, including electron microscopes, ultracentrifuges, nuclear magnetic spectrographs, optical microscopes, and automated sampling devices. Some experiments may call for radioactive tracers. Computer knowledge is becoming more and more essential for work in the life sciences.

Success in biology requires the ability to plan, organize, and direct the work of others; to establish and maintain cooperative working relationships with representatives of numerous agencies and groups; and to analyze situations accurately and make independent recommendations. Verbal ability, both spoken and written, is required.

It should not be too difficult to obtain a job as a life scientist if you have an advanced degree. There should be about 12,000 openings a year.

Employment will increase as a result of more interest in medical research and concern about the environment. As new laws and standards regarding environmental safeguards and testing are passed by legislatures, industry will be required to hire more life scientists. The government, too, will need more skilled technologists to inspect and test the products and wastes given off by factories and industrial plants.

More government and private spending on cancer and medical research is expected in the 1980's. This will create new jobs for microbiologists, biochemists, virologists, laboratory animal keepers, pharmacologists, and so on.

The development of synthetic fuel substitutes, too, will create jobs for biologists, who will have to test the safety of the emissions. Alcohol produced from grain is being considered as a renewable fuel resource. Also, cottonwood-type trees, which grow rapidly, may be used as a heating fuel. Agricultural scientists will be needed to develop better harvesting and processing methods for these crops.

Some of the most interesting environmental careers may not have very many openings. Jobs for wildlife biologists and marine biologists, for instance, are sought after by many more applicants than there are positions. Usually successful candidates have advanced training as well as field experience that they acquired as volunteers and assistants during college. Most life scientists work in well-lighted, well-ventilated, clean laboratories. They usually work 5-day, 35-hour workweeks and have liberal hospital and fringe benefits. Some jobs, however, require strenuous work outdoors under extreme conditions. Other jobs may require arduous around-the-clock data gathering. These jobs are very exciting for the scientists who choose them, and, often, the thrill of creative research is the greatest reward of all.

The U.S. Department of Labor suggests that anyone seeking a career in the life sciences should plan to obtain an advanced degree.

The bachelor's degree is the usual minimum requirement for interesting work in industry or for the Federal government. A life scientist at this level can carry out the research proposed by project leaders or can perform tests, such as examining foods for microorganisms. Promotions, however, usually go to those with higher degrees. Biological sales and service technician jobs can usually be had with a bachelor's degree. Many life scientists begin their careers at the bachelor's level and continue to study toward a master's degree or a PhD. Often this on-the-job training is paid for by the employer.

A master's degree is generally required for any employment that requires independent work, and a doctorate is becoming the minimum degree for research work and university teaching. Most undergraduate and high school teaching jobs also require at least a master's.

High school students who want to prepare for a career in the life sciences should make sure that they have a good foundation in the basic skills before beginning college. English is important, since the written and spoken word is the means by which biologists communicate. The studying of a science requires careful textbook and journal reading, as well as good skills in compositional writing. Research papers and speeches at conferences are the principal means by which scientists learn of each other's work, which is vital for improving their own research.

Computer science and mathematics are essential in today's life science work. Algebra, geometry, trigonometry, and, especially, statistics are the tools that biologists use in analyzing their work. Foreign languages are important for communicating with scientists in other countries and for reading scientific works that are not translated into English.

The social studies courses help you understand the interrelationships between technology, science, economics, and the historical development of mankind.

In high school you should take every science course that is available. Biology, chemistry, and physics are fundamental to your understanding of how living systems operate. If you can also take an ecology or oceanography course, you will find these very useful.

Art and photography are used by biologists to illustrate their research and to record their observations. If you are skilled and trained in these fields, you will have a distinct advantage in the life sciences.

Students planning a career in the life sciences should be able to work independently and as part of a team. They must have a great deal of patience and perseverance, since the work may often be tedious and repetitive. Also, they must not be easily frustrated, since research often leads to "blind alleys" or to inconclusive results. The field may require physical stamina and the ability to endure discomfort.

Inexperienced life scientists with bachelor's degrees start at approximately $16,700; those with master's degrees at approximately $17,500, and those with doctorates at approximately $26,000. The average salary for a biologist in 1982 was $31,900. Specialists in agricultural fields averaged $28,000.

3. Where You Can Obtain Training in the Life Sciences

Most universities and many four-year colleges offer baccalaureate degrees in the life sciences. Some of these are:

Adrian College, Adrian, Michigan 49221
Albion College, Albion, Michigan 49224
Albright College, Reading, Pennsylvania 19604
Allegheny College, Meadville, Pennsylvania 16335
Antioch College, Yellow Springs, Ohio 45387
Bates College, Lewiston, Maine 04240
Bethany College, Bethany, West Virginia 26032
Boston College, Chestnut Hill, Massachusetts 02167
Bowdoin College, Brunswick, Maine 04011
Brandeis University, Waltham, Massachusetts 02154
Brown University, Providence, Rhode Island 02912
Capital University, Columbus, Ohio 43209
Carleton College, Northfield, Minnesota 55057
Central Missouri State University, Warrensburg, Missouri 64093
University of Chicago, Chicago, Illinois 60637
Clark University, Worcester, Massachusetts 01610
Clemson University, Clemson, South Carolina 29631
University of Dayton, Dayton, Ohio 45469

University of Delaware, Newark, Delaware 19711
Earlham College, Richmond, Indiana 47374
East Texas State University, Commerce, Texas 75428
Eastern Michigan University, Ypsilanti, Michigan 48197
University of Evansville, Evansville, Indiana 47702
Florence State University, Florence, Alabama 35630
Fordham University, New York, N.Y. 10021
Furman University, Greenville, South Carolina 29613
Georgetown University, Washington, D.C. 20007
Gettysburg College, Gettysburg, Pennsylvania 17325
Hamilton College, Clinton, New York 13323
Hampton Institute, Hampton, Virginia 23368
Hobart and William Smith College, Geneva, New York 14456
Hofstra University, Hempstead, New York 11550
Kalamazoo College, Kalamazoo, Michigan 49001
Kenyon College, Gambler, Ohio 43022
Lafayette College, Easton, Pennsylvania 18042
Lehigh University, Bethlehem, Pennsylvania 18015
Lycoming College, Williamsport, Pennsylvania 17701
Madison College, Harrisonsburg, Virginia 22801
Marietta College, Marietta, Ohio 45750
Marquette University, Milwaukee, Wisconsin 53233
Miami University, Oxford, Ohio 45056
Muhlenberg College, Allentown, Pennsylvania 18104
New York University, New York, N.Y. 10003
Northeastern University, Boston, Massachusetts 02115
Oberlin College, Oberlin, Ohio 44074
Occidental College, Los Angeles, California 90041
University of Rochester, Rochester, New York 14627
Siena College, Loudonville, New York 12211
Stanford University, Stanford, California 94305
State University of New York, Albany, Binghamton, and Buffalo,
    New York
Trinity College, Hartford, Connecticut 06106
Tufts University, Medford, Massachusetts 02155
Vanderbilt University, Nashville, Tennessee 37240
Villanova University, Villanova, Pennsylvania 19085
University of Washington, Seattle, Washington 98195
Wayne State University, Detroit, Michigan 48202
West Virginia University, Morgantown, West Virginia 26506
Western Kentucky University, Bowling Green, Kentucky 42101
College of Wooster, Wooster, Ohio 44691

4. More Information on Life Science Careers

To obtain information on certain life science careers, write to:

American Institute of Biological Sciences
3900 Wisconsin Avenue, NW
Washington, DC 20016

American Physiological Society
9650 Rockville Pike
Bethesda, MD 20014

Institute of Food Technology
Suite 2120; 221 North LaSalle Street
Chicago, IL 60601

Federation of American Societies for Experimental Biology
9650 Rockville Pike
Bethesda, MD 20014

American Society of Agronomy
677 South Segoe Road
Madison, WI 53711

National Wildlife Federation
1412 16th Street, NW
Washington, DC 20036

Sierra Club
800 Second Avenue
New York, NY 10017

For information about careers for biologists and biochemists in the Federal government, write to:

U.S. Civil Service Commission
1900 E Street, NW
Washington, DC 20415

U.S. Department of Agriculture
Department of Personnel
Washington, DC 20250

For detailed information, read:

Exploring Careers in Science by Stanley Jay Shapiro.
   Richards Rosen Press, Inc.

Your Future in Agribusiness by Chester S. Hutchinson.
   Richards Rosen Press, Inc.

Chapter V

Environmental Engineering Careers

The growth of environmental engineering has been spurred on not only by public concern over environmental pollution but also by several major Federal laws. The earliest environmental engineers were called sanitary engineers, and their duties were much more limited than those of their modern-day counterparts. Environmental engineers must understand the fragility of the environment and the hazards that toxic chemicals and waste products present to people and the environment. Today, petroleum and mining engineers must learn how to tap the resources of our planet without harming the landscape, the water, or the air.

In this chapter you will learn about engineering in general, the education of an engineer, licensing requirements, and opportunities for new entrants. Details are given for fourteen areas of environmental engineering; these include sanitary engineer, hydrologic engineer, water pollution control engineer, industrial water treatment engineer, petroleum engineer, oil pollution control engineer, mining engineer, nuclear engineer, radiation protection engineer, noise engineer, air engineer, agricultural engineer, waste management engineer, and resource recovery engineer.

A. A CAREER AS AN ENVIRONMENTAL ENGINEER

Engineers apply the theories and principles of science and mathematics to practical technical problems. Often their work is the link between a scientific discovery and its useful application. Engineers design machinery, products, systems, and processes for efficient and economical performance. They develop electric power, water supply, and waste disposal systems to meet the problems of urban living. They design industrial machinery and equipment used to manufacture goods, and heating, air-conditioning, and ventilation equipment for more comfortable surroundings. Engineers develop scientific equipment to probe and examine the ocean depths, the air, the earth, and its creatures. They design, plan, and supervise the construction of buildings, highways, and rapid transit systems. They design and develop consumer products such as television sets, refrigerators, and automobiles. They develop systems for the production and manufacture of virtually everything we eat, wear, and work with. Their future accomplishments could help increase energy supplies, develop more pollution-free power and manufacturing plants, and aid science's fight against environmental disaster.

Engineers must consider many factors in developing a new product. For example, laws have been written that require a reduction in pollutants from automobile exhausts. Engineers are assigned the task of designing a low-cost, efficient system for removing these excess waste products. Engineers must work with scientists to determine the general way the device will work. Then they design and test all components, and finally integrate them into the design of the automobile. They must then evaluate the overall effectiveness of the new device, as well as its cost and reliability. This design process applies to most products, including those as different as medical equipment, electronic computers, and wastewater processors.

In addition to design and development, many engineers work in testing, production, operation, or maintenance. They supervise the operation of production processes, determine the causes of breakdowns, and perform tests on newly manufactured products to ensure that quality and environmental standards are maintained. They also estimate the time and cost needed to complete construction and other engineering projects. Still others work in administrative and management jobs where an engineering background is necessary. Engineers with considerable education or experience sometimes work as consultants or teach in the engineering schools of colleges and universities.

Engineers use calculators and computers to solve mathematical equations that help specify what is needed for a device or structure to function in the most efficient manner. They spend a great deal of time writing reports of their findings and consulting with other engineers. Because of the complexity of most of the projects in which they are involved, engineers must be able to work well as part of a team. Engineers should have creativity, an analytical mind, and a capacity for detail.

Most engineers spend a great deal of their time in offices; some are at a desk from nine to five each work day. But some engineers work in research laboratories, factories, or at chemical, water, or power plants. Some engineers may work outdoors part of the time. Many must put in considerable overtime to meet deadlines, often without additional compensation.

Engineers are among the highest-paid professionals. Many 1981 graduates in engineering found positions, especially in the petroleum and mining fields, that offered annual salaries around $25,000. Some experienced engineers in 1981 earned close to $40,000 a year.

Engineering is the largest scientific and technical occupation. In 1981 about 1.25 million persons were employed as engineers. Opportunities are good for employment as an engineer, but some fields may not increase as expected if government research and private development expenditures do not increase. These difficulties can be minimized by selection of training in as broad a field as possible, so that you can switch your specialization to meet the needs of the latest technological developments.

One of the beauties of engineering is that the normal requirement for beginning jobs is only a bachelor's degree in engineering. In a typical four-year curriculum, the first two years are spent studying basic sciences — mathematics, physics, chemistry, and introductory engineering — and the humanities, social sciences, and English. The last two years are devoted, for the most part, to specialized engineering courses.

Some schools have five- or even six-year cooperative plans in which students coordinate classroom study and practical work experience. In addition to gaining useful experience, students can help finance part of their education. Because of the need to keep up with rapid advances in technology, engineers often continue their education throughout their careers. A list of some of the schools that offer engineering degrees is given at the end of this chapter.

All fifty states and the District of Columbia require licensing for engineers whose work may affect life, health, or property or who offer their services to the public. Generally, registration requirements include a degree from an accredited engineering school, four years of relevant work experience, and the passing of a state examination.

Engineering graduates usually begin work under the supervision of experienced engineers. Experienced engineers may advance to positions of greater responsibility, and some move to management or administrative positions. Some engineers obtain graduate degrees in business administration, scientific specialties, law, economics, or environmental fields in order to improve their advancement opportunities and to allow them the ability to move into jobs that they may find more interesting or challenging.

Engineering graduates with a bachelor's degree and no experience averaged $25,200 a year in private industry in 1982; those with a master's degree and no experience, $28,200 a year; and those with a Ph.D., $36,300. The average salary for engineers in the Federal government was about $36,000.

Starting offers for those with bachelor's degrees vary by field, as shown in the following table:

Field	*Starting Salary*
Petroleum engineering	$30,468
Chemical engineering	27,072

Mining engineering 25,368
Metallurgical engineering 25,272
Mechanical engineering 25,176
Electrical engineering 24,768
Nuclear engineering 24,468
Industrial engineering 24,276
Aeronautical engineering 23,676
Civil engineering 23,100

B. CAREERS IN ENVIRONMENTAL ENGINEERING

The occupations in which engineers work that involve protection and development of the environment are subordinate to the nine principal engineering specialties. The largest engineering field is electrical engineering (over 300,000 employed in 1978), followed by industrial (over 200,000), mechanical (over 200,000), civil (over 150,000), chemical (over 50,000), aerospace (over 50,000), petroleum (over 20,000), metallurgical (over 15,000), and mining (around 10,000). Within these major branches are more than eighty-five subdivisions. As was previously discussed, wise students will keep their opportunities as flexible as possible by not narrowing their education toward a specific job, but will prepare themselves for many fields that may offer them jobs or may newly emerge.

The Department of Energy says that there will be a need (•) and a shortage (••) of engineers in the following environmental categories in the 1980's:

Job Categories	Coal	Nuclear	Oil and Gas Exploration and Extraction	Oil Shale	Synthetic Fuel from Coal	Fossil-Fueled Electric Power Plants	Petroleum Refiners
Engineers:							
Chemical		••	••	••	•	•	••
Civil	•	••	••	••	••	•	•
Electrical	•	••	•	•	•	••	•
Industrial	•		•				•
Mechanical	•	••	•	•	•	•	••
Metallurgical		••					•
Mining	•	•	•	•			•
Nuclear		••					
Petroleum			••		•		••

Sanitary Engineer

Sanitary engineers, sometimes known as public health engineers, work in a variety of areas. They design and direct construction and operation of projects such as waterworks, wastewater treatment plants, and other sanitary facilities. Some sanitary engineers work with sewage disposal, water pollution control, or water supply. Sanitary engineers also work in the development of watersheds and direct the building of aqueducts, filtration plants, and storage and distribution systems for water supplies in some states.

Some sanitary engineers work in environmental protection programs and might investigate complex problems such as the pollution of a stream. To do this, they might make detailed engineering investigations and studies of sewage and industrial waste treatment. They would investigate conditions in public waterways, industrial plants, public and private sewer systems, industrial waste treatment plants, and sewage disposal plants. This work may involve collecting samples, making flow measurements, and preparing detailed reports, sketches, plans, and diagrams of factors affecting the pollution problem. The engineer must then evaluate the condition of treatment facilities and the effectiveness of the treatment process.

Sanitary engineers may plan and supervise the engineering, construction, and operation of all sewage and industrial waste treatment projects and municipal water supply programs.

Sanitary engineers must be able to learn and apply basic engineering principles and methods to water pollution control problems. They must be able to plan and organize their work independently and to exercise judgment in evaluating situations and making decisions. They must present technical material in reports clearly and concisely.

There are many opportunities for qualified sanitary engineers. Communities must comply with more stringent clean-water requirements; this means expansion of existing wastewater treatment facilities and construction of new plants.

To become a sanitary engineer you must combine engineering training with a knowledge of the health sciences including biology, chemistry, bacteriology, and physics. You must also have a knowledge of the equipment and operation of water, solid waste, and sewage treatment plants and systems.

Hydrologic Engineer

These engineers design and direct construction of power and other projects involving the control and use of water. They work on many projects — artificial canals, dams, reservoirs, booster stations, and flood control programs. They work in research and study problems such as soil drainage, conservation, and flooding.

Hydrologic engineers are civil engineers. They have specialized training in how to build structures that control water flow. They can examine existing facilities or design new ones with teams of other water experts.

They may work on dams, bridges, culverts, retaining walls, fills, pipe crossings, or channel improvements. Some work with the U.S. Weather Bureau in flood forecasting and with municipalities on flood control. They may specialize in analyzing drought conditions, rainfall, watersheds, and in examining possible flood runoff areas.

Some hydrologic engineers work with farmers in constructing irrigation projects to distribute water to agricultural lands. These specialists are sometimes called irrigation engineers.

The conservation and distribution of water, as well as the use of water to turn electric generators and to cool nuclear facilities should mean more jobs for hydrologic engineers.

EXXON PHOTO

Hydrologic engineers install pipe on an irrigation project.

Water Pollution Control Engineer

The protection of our water is the water pollution control engineers' job. They examine and analyze engineering and construction plans, such as water supply systems and plants, industrial and wastewater treatment systems, and collection systems, to see that they meet all the requirements and regulations foi protecting the water supply. Once the site has been approved, these engineers might inspect the installation, as well as its surroundings, to check that no pollution is occurring.

One of their most important responsibilities is to advise management, operators, and officials on pollution problems and how to handle them.

The Clean Water Act of 1977 requires that municipalities, industries, and power companies carefully monitor and control their water emissions. Large companies hire water pollution control engineers to help them meet the requirements of the Act.

State, regional, and Federal agencies use these engineers to inspect treatment plants and industrial water users to verify compliance with the law. These engineers recommend issuance or denial of National Pollution Control permits, which permit construction and operation of facilities.

They work with government representatives and planning agencies to discuss water pollution problems, and they work with consulting engineers of major plants before any major changes are approved.

Water pollution control engineers must know the laws, codes, and regulations of pollution control, as well as having a knowledge of chemistry and bacteriology. They must know about the treatment and handling of water, sewage, and liquid waste. Normally, a professional engineer's license is required for this occupation.

Industrial Water Treatment Engineer

Water as it comes from the tap is often unacceptable for industrial use and must be given additional treatment. Products such as food, beverages, and drugs often require water purification standards above those provided by municipal water suppliers. Water also plays an important part in the operation and maintenance of machinery and equipment; improperly treated water can cause deterioration.

Some chemical engineers specialize in water treatment processes used in industrial production. They develop specialized water treatment processes and chemical treatments to suit industrial needs.

They develop water treatment plans to solve water quality problems. Where water is part of a food product or beverage, for example, industrial water treatment engineers may have to develop a cost-efficient method for treating a taste problem. Or, if they were working for an industrial plant, they might have to find a way to screen out small particulate matter in the water that might cause breakdown or corrosion in the machinery.

Petroleum Engineer

Petroleum engineers are involved in exploring and drilling for oil and gas. They determine and develop the best and most efficient methods for recovering oil and gas from a petroleum reservoir.

When a new pool of raw petroleum is found, it can usually be pumped by traditional methods; however, the monetary incentive to find fuel has sparked research and development of many unusual methods. So-called "dry wells," where it was once unprofitable to remove the remaining oil, are being flooded with hot water and detergents to force the oil to the surface: however, half the oil is still left in the ground. New oil finds in Antarctica or in turbulent deep seas will provide constant challenges for these engineers.

Petroleum engineers work with exploration geologists, chemists, other scientists, and environmentalists to increase the production of oil in a safe, efficient, ecological way. Their work can make a significant contribution to increasing available energy supplies. They will continue to develop methods for recovering petroleum that are cleaner and less harmful to the environment. Offshore drilling rigs have been constructed so that they encourage marine life, instead of destroying it.

COURTESY PHILLIPS PETROLEUM COMPANY
Petroleum engineers at work.

Petroleum engineers work for the major oil companies and smaller independent oil exploration and production companies. They also work for the manufacturers that produce drilling equipment and supplies. Some petroleum engineers work as consultants to banks and financial institutions, which need their knowledge of the economic value of oil and gas properties.

About three-fourths of all petroleum engineers are employed in the oil-producing states of Texas, Oklahoma, Louisiana, and California. Many work overseas in oil-producing companies.

Political and economic developments will require increasing supplies of petroleum and natural gas from Western countries, despite energy conservation measures. With efforts to attain energy self-sufficiency and with high petroleum prices, increasingly sophisticated recovery methods will be used. New sources of oil, such as oil shale, and new offshore oil resources will be developed. Also, new drilling techniques for developing geothermal energy will be needed. There is also the greater concern of oil companies to protect the environment, which will require improved drilling and pumping techniques. All of these factors will contribute to an increasing demand for petroleum engineers.

Oil Pollution Control Engineer

The "oil spill" is a major concern of the oil industry. The ever-increasing demand for petroleum products has to be met without risking the environment. Although oil spills cannot be entirely prevented, steps are being taken by oil pollution control engineers to reduce the probability that they will occur. They have redesigned pipelines, oil rigs, tankers, tank trucks, valves, and other hardware used to contain and ship petroleum so that oil will not leak out accidentally.

These engineers continually check and monitor oil pumping and shipping, using advanced surveillance equipment incorporating ultrasonics, X rays, and television. They closely follow such information as tides, currents, winds, and weather to prevent accidents. They determine procedures for the inspection of underground pipelines as well as surface equipment. They use advanced computer programs to provide twenty-four-hour protection, which will automatically stop the flow of petroleum if a leak occurs.

No perfect control or cleanup method exists, but oil pollution engineers are continually improving the methods they use. When a major spill is discovered, containment of the oil is the most important single action that can be taken. The engineer must decide on the best strategy and the methods to be used in a particular spill while considering such factors as wind direction and velocity, sea conditions, towing loads, shape and density of the slick, and so on. Directing the control and cleanup of a major spill requires working under difficult conditions because spills can occur during stormy weather and away from land.

Another responsibility for these engineers is to plan training programs for crews so that they can quickly react in an emergency. They must also schedule regular drills to be sure that machinery and equipment are in good working order and that personnel are properly trained.

Oil pollution control engineers work with local fire departments and other municipal agencies so that proper procedures can be implemented to protect citizens, domestic animals, plants, and wildlife from the hazards of an oil spill. Oil spills can affect drinking water, storm water drains, irrigation systems, marinas, swimming beaches, wildlife sanctuaries, tidal basins, and other sensitive areas.

These engineers work for petroleum companies and for Federal and state agencies concerned with the prevention, control, cleanup, and disposal of oil spills. There should be opportunities in this field throughout the 1980's for highly qualified and experienced engineers.

Mining Engineer

Mining engineers find, extract, and prepare minerals for industry to use. They design open-pit and underground mines, supervise the construction of mine shafts and tunnels, and devise methods for transporting minerals to processing plants. They are responsible for the efficient and economical operation of mines and mine safety — including ventilation, water supply, power, communications, and equipment maintenance.

Some mining engineers work with geologists and metallurgical engineers to locate and appraise new ore deposits. Others develop new mining equipment or direct mineral processing operations, which involve separating minerals from the dirt, rock, and other minerals with which they are mixed.

Mining engineers, today, are concerned with protecting the environment as they develop ore deposits. Unsightly strip mining is carried out under contracts with municipal governments that require restoration of the land after the minerals are removed. Pollution and wastes from the mines are carefully treated so that they do not harm the air and the water supply. Contaminated areas are being reclaimed. Mining companies are encouraging their engineers to find improved methods that will use less energy and do less harm to the surroundings.

Mining engineers are usually employed at the location of mineral deposits, often near small communities. However, those in research, teaching, management, consulting, or sales often work in metropolitan areas.

These engineers frequently specialize in the mining of one specific mineral such as coal or copper. Efforts to attain energy self-sufficiency should spur the demand for coal and therefore increase the need for mining engineers. Rare metal finds in the Southwest and Alaska have brought millions of dollars into development of these resources. Chromium and molybdenum have previously been mined outside the United States, but now new finds are encouraging domestic companies. Also the price of minerals such as gold has encouraged the reopening of some mines. New techniques also have made economically unfeasible operations profitable again.

Metallurgical engineers are finding new uses for alloys that should increase the demand for less widely used ores. And the recovery of minerals from the seafloor should present major challenges as well as opportunities to the mineral engineer.

Nuclear Engineer and Radiation Protection Engineer

Nuclear energy is a source of heat and radiation that can be used for peaceful as well as military purposes. Although peaceful applications have been expanding rapidly in recent years, they are still in the early stages of development. Nuclear energy is a cost-effective method of producing electricity; however, the dangers of the plant are still being examined and are not fully understood. Continuing research and development will be needed during the next several decades to find newer, safer, and more efficient ways of utilizing this energy.

Nuclear engineers are involved in many aspects of this developing industry. They are involved in the processes for exploring, mining, milling, and refining uranium-bearing ores. They develop methods and equipment for the production of nuclear fuels. They design nuclear reactors, reactor components, and nuclear instruments. They prescribe the operation and maintenance of nuclear facilities. They devise methods for disposing of radioisotopes and spent fuel rods, and they work on the production of nuclear weapons.

Nuclear engineers are specially trained in nuclear technology, but most have experience and education in related engineering fields. Most are mechanical engineers, but many electrical, electronic, chemical, civil, and metallurgical engineers work in this field. Many of the engineers do research and development work; others work on design and operation of nuclear reactors, nuclear instruments, and other equipment.

Responsibility for radiation safety at a nuclear power generating plant rests with the radiation protection engineer, who supervises a number of technicians. These experts are responsible for monitoring the chemistry, radiochemistry, and radiation protection programs at the plant. They evaluate the reactor plant water that is heated by the nuclear reaction to see that it is safe within the standards imposed by the industry. They prepare reports on the plant operation, the radioactive waste released, and the environmental monitoring that occurs in the water, air, and community surrounding the facility. They are responsible for developing emergency procedures and for training plant personnel.

Because of the continuing controversy over nuclear power plant safety in the United States, openings for nuclear engineers were few in the mid-1980's. However, Europe and Japan have increased their dependence on nuclear power and are continuing to build new facilities.

Noise Engineer

Noise, or acoustical, engineers use engineering know-how to protect our hearing by reducing noise from transportation, construction equipment, power plants, factories, and other sources. They work with noise specialists and physicists.

To examine excess noise, these engineers set up noise-measurement equipment to monitor various sites. Then, using statistical methods and computer analysis, they pinpoint the source of the noise and recommend control procedures.

Sometimes an examination of engineering plans can lead to a minor alteration in construction that will greatly reduce excess noise. Sometimes they recommend noise barriers to absorb or reflect sound waves. Often they suggest a total redesign of a machine to make it run quieter.

Noise engineers usually have a background in engineering coupled with training in physics. Knowledge of medicine, physiology, and psychology are helpful for understanding the mechanism of hearing and the effects of noise. They are employed by airports, power plants, manufacturers, research organizations, and government agencies. Currently there is a need for noise engineers, and the demand is expected to increase as people become more aware of the importance of noise control.

Air Engineer

Air engineers or air quality engineers try to keep the air fit to breathe. They help in the design and construction of factories and power plants so that pollutants are carefully controlled. They may design machinery or special filters to clean exhaust fumes, and they monitor the air over cities to check on its quality.

Air engineers decide where and how often air testing should be done, set up equipment, and train air technicians to run tests. They collect all the test results for computer processing, analyze the findings, and report their recommendations.

To prevent new pollution, plans for construction that may add pollutants to the air are analyzed by air engineers. They must consider the new designs along with information on wind direction, climate, population, traffic, housing, contours of the land, and so on.

Some air engineers are working on stopping pollution at its sources by developing new industrial processes, finding methods for removing sulfur from fuels, or designing engines that are more efficient and burn cleaner.

Air engineers are usually trained on the job. They become skilled in methods of measuring and controlling air pollution. They learn about the nature and extent of pollutants and the processes that produce them, as well as the economic, environmental, and health effects of such pollutants. They must also become familiar with Federal, state, and local air pollution laws and regulations.

Air engineers work for city, county, state, and Federal agencies. They are also employed by industries that have air pollution problems, such as chemical plants, steel mills, and foundries.

New air regulations have created a demand for air engineers, who make it possible for industries to meet the regulations. However, there will probably be few openings after the mid-1980's.

Agricultural Engineer

Agricultural engineers design agricultural machinery and equipment and develop methods that will improve the production, processing, and distribution of food and other agricultural products. They are also concerned with the conservation and management of energy, soil, and water resources.

Agricultural engineers work for manufacturers of farm equipment, electric utility companies, and distributors of farm equipment and supplies. Some work as consultants who supply services to farmers; others may specialize in one branch of farming such as dairy farming, cereal farming, and so on.

The increasing demand for agricultural products, the modernization of farm operations, the increasing emphasis on conservation of resources, and the use of agricultural products and wastes as industrial raw materials and energy sources should provide good opportunities for engineers who want to specialize in applying their skills to agribusiness.

Waste Management Engineer and Resource Recovery Engineer

Engineers in the fields are experts in waste handling, processing, disposal, and resource recovery systems. A huge saving in both dollars and energy can be made if wastes are either efficiently removed or, better, reused by our industrial society.

The waste management engineer must first see that solid waste disposal methods are safe, sanitary, and nonpolluting. He or she must make sure that all sanitary codes and laws are enforced. The engineer may work as a consultant in the design of a plant, factory, or waste disposal facility to check that the most up-to-date methods are being employed. Most engineers in this field plan and conduct research projects for the development of new methods and technologies for the treatment of wastes.

Resource recovery is a new but increasingly important field. Waste paper and aluminum recovery efforts in particular have been very successful. However, the complex technology for recovery of energy and other valuable resources is still experimental.

Engineers who specialize in resource recovery are usually active in the promotion of this new field. They aid in the design of resource recovery facilities and monitor ones already in operation. They do research on chemical and mechanical resource recovery technology — investigating new techniques and evaluating the economic and practical gains.

These jobs will be increasingly in demand. Currently sanitary landfill is the best method for solid waste disposal, but soon resource recovery technology advances will offer feasible alternatives.

C. WHERE YOU CAN OBTAIN TRAINING IN ENGINEERING

Many universities offer baccalaureate degrees in engineering. Some of these are:

Bucknell University, Lewisburg, Pennsylvania 17837

California State University, Long Beach, Chico, Fresno, Sacramento, San Diego, San Jose, Northridge, Los Angeles, California

Catholic University, Washington, D.C. 20017
Christian Brothers College, Memphis, Tennessee 38104
Colorado State University, Fort Collins, Colorado 80521
University of Detroit, Detroit, Michigan 48221
Drexel University, Philadelphia, Pennsylvania 19104
Gannon College, Erie, Pennsylvania 16505
University of Hawaii, Honolulu, Hawaii 96822
Howard University, Washington, D.C. 20001
University of Idaho, Moscow, Idaho 83843
Iowa State University, Ames, Iowa 50010
Lamar University, Beaumont, Texas 77710
Loyola University, Los Angeles, California 90045
University of Massachusetts, Amherst, Massachusetts 01002
Massachusetts Institute of Technology, Cambridge, Massachusetts 02139
Monmouth College, West Long Branch, New Jersey 07764
University of New Hampshire, Durham, New Hampshire 03824
New Mexico State University, Las Cruces, New Mexico 88003
University of North Carolina, Chapel Hill, North Carolina 27514
University of Notre Dame, Notre Dame, Indiana 46556
Ohio University, Athens, Ohio 45701
Oregon State University, Corvallis, Oregon 97331
University of Pittsburgh, Pittsburgh, Pennsylvania 15213
Princeton University, Princeton, New Jersey 08540
Southern Illinois University, Edwardsville, Indiana 62025
Southern Methodist University, Dallas, Texas 75275
St. Louis University, St. Louis, Missouri 63103
Syracuse University, Syracuse, New York 13210
Texas A & I University, Kingsville, Texas 78363
Tufts University, Medford, Massachusetts 02155
Union College, Schenectady, New York 12308
University of Utah, Salt Lake City, Utah 84112
Vanderbilt University, Nashville, Tennessee 37240
University of Virginia, Charlottesville, Virginia 22903
Virginia Polytechnical Institute, Blacksburg, Virginia 24061
Widener College, Chester, Pennsylvania 19013
University of Wisconsin, Madison, Milwaukee, Plattesville, Wisconsin

D. MORE INFORMATION ON ENGINEERING CAREERS

For general and specific information on engineering, write to:

Engineers' Council for Professional Development
345 East 47th Street
New York, NY 10017

Engineering Manpower Commission
Engineers Joint Council
345 East 47th Street
New York, NY 10017

National Society of Professional Engineers
2029 K Street, NW
Washington, DC 20006

American Society of Agricultural Engineers
2950 Niles Road
St. Joseph, MI 49085

American Institute of Chemical Engineers
345 East 47th Street
New York, NY 10017

American Society of Civil Engineers
345 East 47th Street
New York, NY 10017

The Society of Mining Engineers
Caller Number D
Littleton, CO 80123

Society of Petroleum Engineers
6200 North Central Expressway
Dallas, TX 75206

Society of Women Engineers
345 East 47th Street
New York, NY 10017

American Society of Engineering Education
One Dupont Circle
Suite 400
Washington DC 20036

For detailed information, read:

Agricultural Engineer. Careers, Publisher.
Mining Engineer. Chronicle Guidance Publications, Inc.
Engineers Unlimited: Your Careers in Engineering by Harry E. Neal. J. Messner, Publisher.
Engineering Is Like This by Bertha Sanford Dodge. Little, Brown, Publishers.

Chapter VI

Environmental Scientists

This chapter discusses four professions that are directly involved in helping us understand our natural environment. You will learn about geologists, who study the structure, composition, and history of the earth's crust; geophysicists, who study the composition and physical aspects of the earth and its electric, magnetic, and gravitational fields; meteorologists, who study the weather and the atmosphere; and oceanographers, who study the sea. In this chapter details are given on how to prepare for these professions, facts about the work these scientists perform, and information on job opportunities. Nine specializations in geology, ten in geophysics, eight in meteorology, and five in oceanography are discussed.

A. CAREERS IN GEOLOGY

Geology is the study of the earth. Geologists try to understand how the earth was formed and how it changes. They study rocks, soils, mountains, rivers, oceans, caves, glaciers, and other parts of the earth.

The earth was formed more than 4½ billion years ago. It has changed in many ways since then. Many of the changes occur slowly and will continue as long as the planet exists. Diastrophism is the geologic term that covers all the various forces that have caused the earth's crust to be deformed, producing continents, mountains, valleys, chasms, and so on. Earthquakes and volcanic eruptions have changed huge pieces of land, forming mountains out of deserts and causing islands to surface above the sea. Erosion from wind and rain has flattened craggy peaks into farmlands, and glaciers have carved U-shaped valleys through mountains of granite.

Water also changes the earth. Waves can wash away shorelines in one area of the earth and deposit new land in other regions. Rivers eat away mountains piece by piece, carrying the soil downriver to form enriched deltas, such as Mississippi and Egypt.

Some geologists study the remains of animals and plants that lived thousands of years ago. Their skeletons and imprints have become fossils, which tell us how life evolved on the earth.

Geology is usually subdivided into various fields of specialization, but each field is intimately related to the others. Geophysics is the study of earthquakes, the earth's magnetism, the heat flow within the earth, the earth's gravity, and the earth's interior. Geochemistry is the study of the chemical composition of the earth, its rocks and minerals. Historical geology is the study of the sequence of events that have occurred during the formation of the continents and oceans. Structural geology is the study of how the rocks and land formations were deformed and changed throughout the earth's history. Stratigraphy is the study of rocks formed from oceanic deposits, which can reveal the succession of biologic and geologic events. Geomorphology is the study of the earth's landforms. Paleontology is the study of fossils. Paleoecology is the study of ancient plant and animal communities. Economic geology is the study of ore-forming minerals and fuel deposits that can be mined or developed for industrial uses.

Geologists study the earth's crust by examining rocks that they find on the surface and by drilling into the earth to recover rock cores. They identify rocks and minerals by testing them for hardness, density, color, microscopic details, and radioactivity and by analyzing them chemically.

Geologists use many tools and instruments such as hammers, chisels, levels, telescopes, electron and optical microscopes, gravity meters, cameras, compasses, and seismographs. They may analyze photomicrographs of a single rock, or they may examine river basin photographs taken from a satellite. The computer is becoming as important a tool for the geologist as it is for the other sciences.

Many geologists work in laboratories, where they carefully examine specimens found in the field by their associates. They test these specimens for physical and chemical properties. They may study fossil remains of animal and vegetable life. They might test the porosity of rocks by dripping oil or water though them. They may examine long core segments of an ocean bottom to determine what kind of life has swum in the ocean above over the last ten thousand years. Special equipment, such as the X-ray diffractometer, tells scientists how the molecules of a mineral crystallized.

Geologists are also called on to advise construction, environmental, and government agencies. They help plan the location of buildings, dams, and highways. Seemingly solid land may have a river flowing a few yards underneath or may be located near an earthquake fault. This information, when available, can save great expense and may avert disaster.

Some geologists administer and manage research and exploration work for the government or for mining or oil companies. Others may teach and work on research projects in colleges and universities.

Mineralogist

Minerals are the pure compounds within and on the earth's surface. They are the source of the metals used by industry and society. Mineralogists are concerned with identifying and classifying all of the crystalline mineral compounds that are found at the earth's surface, within the earth's crust, in lunar and Martian materials, and in meteorites. Mineralogists determine the chemical elements that make up each mineral. They find the structural arrangement of the atoms within the crystal, using electron microscopes and X-ray spectrographs. They measure the physical properties of the mineral and try to discover the possible ways in which it may have been formed.

Petrologist

Petrologists study the composition, classification, and origin of rocks. Rocks are mixtures of many materials, including minerals, fossils, and others. If a rock was formed by cooling from molten, liquid earth, called magma, it is called an igneous rock. If it was formed at regular earth temperatures by the accumulation of mineral grains or by settling particles in lakes or the ocean, it is called a sedimentary rock. The third kind of rock is called metamorphic rock; these rocks were formed from sedimentary or igneous rocks that were subjected to heat and pressure sufficiently great that the crystal structure of the rock changed. Most petrologists specialize in either sedimentary, igneous, or metamorphic petrology. Ninety-five percent of the rocks on the earth's surface are sedimentary, and all of the oil and natural gas deposits are found in sedimentary rocks. Therefore sedimentary petrology is an excellent career. Igneous and metamorphic petrologists are concerned with rocks formed under high temperature or high pressure or both. Many of these rocks are deep within the earth. Petrologists use chemical analysis, X-ray crystallography, special petrographic microscopy, spectrographs, and, of course, the computer.

Economic Geologist

The economic geologist applies a broad knowledge of all branches of geology to the discovery, exploration, development, and exploitation of mineral deposits. This scientist works closely with other professionals such as the engineer, the physicist, the geophysicist, the geochemist, the statistician, and the economist to determine if and how a mineral or fuel discovery can be developed. For this career, sound business principles is an essential requirement.

Marine Geologist

A marine geologist studies the geology of the ocean basins. These shipboard scientists describe, measure, and analyze the structures on and below the seafloor. Most specialize in particular areas such as deepwater environments, continental shelf environments, or coastal environments. Many rich oil fields have been found just off the continental shelfs of North America and northern Europe through studies by these experts. Rich mineral deposits and geothermal energy may be found under the oceans, which cover three-fourths of the planet's surface.

Geochemist

Geochemists study the earth and related planetary bodies from the standpoint of chemistry. They perform the analyses that determine the elements and compounds of rocks, minerals, and ores. Geochemists work with sensitive instruments to examine the finds sent to them by geologists in the field.

Geothermal Geologist

Geothermal geologists are interested in the heat within the earth, especially where it can be exploited by man. This heat generally occurs near or within igneous rocks. Sometimes water flows through these rocks, producing geysers and geothermal springs. Countries with geothermal resources, such as Iceland, have already tapped this "free" energy for heating and for production of electricity.

Geomorphologist

Geomorphologists are specially trained geologists who are interested in land formations, such as mountains, valleys, canyons, and plains. Geomorphology, which is closely associated with geography and topographic mapmaking, is becoming more important as the U.S. is becoming more aware of environmental factors in planning cities, recreation areas, and the exploitation of its mineral welath. Geomorphologists determine how fresh water is distributed on and below the land surface, they study the effects of erosion on the land, and they are concerned with the regeneration of natural conditions after a mine or oil field runs out of its riches. Much geomorphology involves aerial photography and surveying skills, as well as the other tools of the geoscientist.

Petroleum Geologist and Engineering Geologist

Petroleum geologists search for and recover oil and natural gas. Some petroleum geologists work near drilling sites; others, using computers, correlate petroleum-related geologic information for entire regions, so that new sites may be discovered. These scientists carefully study an area, noting its topography, its underlying rock structure, and other geophysical data. They set off explosions underground and record, with a seismograph, the kinds of vibrations sent through the earth. Sound travels faster through rock than through natural gas or oil pools. If they decide to drill an exploratory hole, then, in cooperation with engineering geologists, they must determine the pressure, temperature, viscosity, and chemical composition of the material they hope to extract. Basic research is also being carried out by petroleum geologists with geochemists to try to understand how petroleum is produced by nature, how it can be recovered from oil shale, and how it might be manufactured synthetically.

Where Geologists Work

More than 60 percent of the geologists employed in this country work in private industry. Most work for petroleum companies. Others work for mining and quarrying companies. Some are employed as consultants to construction firms that build roads, tunnels, and dams as well as housing and office developments.

Geologists who work for petroleum companies usually explore for gas and oil. The majority are employed in the United States, but many work in other oil-producing areas such as Canada, Australia, the Middle East, and Indonesia. They do field mapping, make stratigraphic measurements, conduct seismic and gravimetric tests, and perform other geophysical studies. They also work in laboratories doing basic research.

Mining companies use geologists to determine the location and extent of ore reserves in established mining areas, as well as to locate new deposits. Many of these mines are in the Southwest of the United States, Alaska, and in other countries of the world such as South Africa, Brazil, and Chile.

Real-estate developers, banks, and investment firms employ geologists as consultants to help them evaluate properties. Railroads, chemical companies, ceramics firms, and utilities hire geologists to help them find new resources and to prepare for the future.

The Federal government employs geologists. Most work for the Department of the Interior at the U.S. Geological Survey. Others work for the Bureau of Reclamation, the Bureau of Mines, and the Federal Water Pollution Control Administration. The National Park Service also employs geologists. The Department of Agriculture, the National Oceanic and Atmospheric Administration, and the Army Corps of Engineers each have geologists who work with research teams in specialized areas. The National Aeronautics and Space Administration is the latest bureau of the Federal government to use the services of highly trained geologists.

State and local governments, too, employ geologists. They work at local and regional geological survey departments and highway departments and participate in environmental planning.

Schools offer teaching jobs ranging from graduate-level faculty to junior high school earth science teacher. About 400 universities and colleges give degrees in one of the fields of geology, and at least 200 community colleges and 400 four-year colleges offer coursework in geology. In all, these postsecondary schools employ over 4,000 persons to teach geology and related subjects. There are also about 16,000 secondary school teachers who are teaching courses in the earth sciences, although many cannot be considered geologists.

Consulting geologists are in business for themselves. They usually specialize in the geology of a particular area or have special skills, such as in the interpretation of aerial photographs, which makes them valuable for mineral or fuel resource exploration to engineering concerns or to industry.

Some geologists work for nonprofit research institutions, and others are employed by museums.

Employment of geologists is concentrated in those states with large mineral and oil deposits. Almost two-thirds of all geologists work in five states: Texas, California, Louisiana, Colorado, and Oklahoma. Some are employed by American firms overseas for varying periods of time.

How You Can Train for a Job in Geology

Most positions in the geological sciences require a minimum of a master's degree. Research jobs and university teaching require a PhD. Some jobs, particularly in the Federal government, can be found for geologists with a bachelor's degree, but these are becoming scarce. Therefore, you really need a strong academic interest if you want to become a geologist.

The education of a geologist depends on his or her area of specialization. A vertebrate paleontologist, for example, needs a strong background in zoology, comparative anatomy, and, in addition to general geology courses, coursework in paleontology. A petroleum geologist should have training in physical and inorganic chemistry, physics, engineering, and special courses in fluid dynamics, as well as his general geology work.

In high school, a future geologist should take as many mathematics and science courses as possible. Algebra, geometry, trigonometry, biology, chemistry, and physics are essential. Besides these, you can take earth science, astronomy, calculus, and advanced placement courses. If your school offers a course in computer programming, this would be a great help.

Take enough English so that you can express yourself clearly in writing and in speech. Great discoveries are of little benefit if no one else can learn about them.

About 400 colleges and universities offer a bachelor's degree in geology. Students studying for this major devote about one-fourth of their time to geology courses such as physical, structural, and historical geology, mineralogy, petrology, and paleontology. About one-third of their coursework is in the basic sciences such as chemistry, physics, and biology; mathematics, including statistics, calculus, differential equations, and computer science; and engineering. The remainder of their study time is engaged in English and composition courses, history and economics, foreign language, and other academic subjects.

More than 160 universities award advanced degrees in geology. Graduate students take advanced courses in geology and specialize in one branch of the science. Students seeking the doctorate do a research dissertation project under the guidance of expert faculty members.

In many of the industrial and government jobs in geology, a person with a bachelor's or master's degree will be specially trained on the job in the unique skills necessary for that occupation. Often, part-time studies leading to a graduate degree are paid for by the employer to enhance the knowledge and usefulness of the scientist.

Geologists usually begin their careers in field exploration or as research assistants in laboratories. With experience, they can be promoted to project leader, program manager, or other management and research positions.

Students planning careers in exploration geology and in some of the other fields where vigorous mountaineering, hiking, or other scouting-type skills are needed should like the outdoors and must have physical stamina.

Opportunities for Geologists

Employment opportunities in geology, as in the other sciences and all professions, vary with the general economic climate of the country and with the nation's needs. The long-range picture looks very good. Dwindling energy, mineral, and water resources, increasing environmental concerns, a better use of land, and a need for better waste disposal systems present new challenges to our society. The geologist will serve a special and important function in reaching an energy-independent, ecologically balanced future in the twenty-first century.

The employment of geologists is expected to grow faster than the average for all occupations. Over 2,300 new jobs for geologists are expected each year.

The demand for qualified women geologists is very high, and there is no reason why women should not find a geological career extremely rewarding. There are also very few minority groups represented in the occupation. Therefore, many employers are actively recruiting female and minority earth scientists.

If you are interested in geology but would prefer not being a scientist, there are jobs for technical writers and librarians with specialized training in geology. In addition, careers in law or business frequently can be strengthened by a background in geology.

The increased prices for petroleum and the necessity to locate new sources of other minerals as older sources become exhausted will require many new geologists. Additional geologists also will be needed to develop new resources, such as geothermal energy. This, in turn, should require that colleges and universities, which are not hiring many new geology faculty at this time, begin recruiting new instructional staff. The interest in energy resources may also spark school boards into creating new curricula in the earth sciences, which will need trained faculty.

In 1982 average starting salaries for geologists with bachelor's degrees were over $23,800. Graduates with master's degrees started over $29,000, and those with doctorates started over $32,500. The average salary for experienced geologists in 1982 was $33,000.

Where You Can Obtain Training in Geology

University of Alabama, University, Alabama 35486
Allegheny College, Meadville, Pennsylvania 16335
University of Arkansas, Fayetteville, Arkansas 72701
Boston College, Chestnut Hill, Massachusetts 02167
Brown University, Providence, Rhode Island 02912
University of Colorado, Boulder, Colorado 80302
Dartmouth College, Hanover, New Hampshire 03755
University of Dayton, Dayton, Ohio 45469
Dickinson College, Carlisle, Pennsylvania 17013
Hofstra University, Hempstead, New York 11550
Indiana State University, Terre Haute, Indiana 47809
University of Iowa, Iowa City, Iowa 52242
University of Kentucky, Lexington, Kentucky 40506
Long Island University, Brooklyn, N.Y. 11201
Marshall University, Huntington, West Virginia 25705
University of Miami, Coral Gables, Florida 33124
Michigan State University, East Lansing, Michigan 48824
University of Montana, Missoula, Montana 59801
University of Nevada, Las Vegas, Nevada 89109

New Mexico Institute of Mining and Technology, Socorro, New
   Mexico 87801
University of North Dakota, Grand Forks, North Dakota 58201
Ohio State University, Columbus, Ohio 43212
Pennsylvania State University, University Park, Pennsylvania 16802
University of Rochester, Rochester, New York 14627
Smith College, Northampton, Massachusetts 01060
St. Louis University, St. Louis, Missouri 63103
Stanford University, Stanford, California 94305
Temple University, Philadelphia, Pennsylvania 19122
Texas A & M University, College Station, Texas 77843
University of Toledo, Toledo, Ohio 43614
Tulane University, New Orleans, Louisiana 70118
Utah State University, Logan, Utah 84322
Virginia Polytechnical Institute, Blacksburg, Virginia 24061
West Virginia University, Morgantown, West Virginia 26506
Western State College, Gunnison, Colorado 81230
College of William and Mary, Williamsburg, Virginia 23185
Williams College, Williamstown, Massachusetts 01267

More Information on Geology Careers
For additional information write to:

   The American Geological Institute
   5205 Leesburg Pike
   Falls Church, VA 22041

For information about Federal government jobs in geology, write to:

   U.S. Civil Service Commission
   1900 E Street NW
   Washington, DC 20415

For detailed information about the field, read:
   Your Future in Geology by Joseph L. Weitz. Richards Rosen Press,
Inc.

B. CAREERS IN GEOPHYSICS

   Geophysics is the application of physics, chemistry, and mathematics
to the problems and processes of the earth. Geophysicists study the
causes and outcomes of natural upheavals such as earthquakes and
volcanoes. They investigate the magnetic and gravitational forces of the

earth. They measure the size and shape of the earth's surface, and they try to locate areas where rich mineral and fuel deposits can be found. The upper atmosphere, the ionosphere, the sun, and the solar system are areas of interest to the geophysicist.

Geophysics is usually divided into three general areas: solid earth geophysics, fluid earth geophysics, and upper atmosphere geophysics. Geophysicists usually specialize in one of these three fields.

Solid earth geophysicists search for oil and mineral deposits, map the earth's surface, and study earthquakes. They are concerned with the geological and planetary aspects of the earth.

Fluid earth geophysicists study the distribution, circulation, and physical properties of underground and surface waters, including glaciers, snow, and permafrost (the perennially frozen subsoil of the arctic tundra). The fluid earth geophysicists are concerned with how rainfall permeates the soil and its effect on water supply, irrigation, flooding, and soil erosion.

Upper atmosphere geophysicists study the earth's magnetic and electric fields. They compare their findings with those from other planets to learn about the history and composition of the solar system. Their research enables meteorologists to make better predictions concerning the weather.

Geophysics is one of the earth sciences. It uses basic scientific principles to study the earth's crust, atmosphere, and water flow. Most of its efforts today are directed toward finding new oil-producing areas. The study of geophysical problems requires a good foundation in chemistry, physics, and mathematics.

Geophysicists study the earth with highly complex instrument such as the magnetometer, which measures variations in the earth's magnetic field; the gravimeter, which measures minute changes in the earth's gravitational attraction; seismographs, which measure the sound waves produced by earthquakes and other disturbances beneath the earth's surface; and satellites, which conduct tests in outer space. The computer, as in all the other sciences today, is a basic tool required for collecting and analyzing data.

The American Geophysical Union, an organization of geophysicists and other scientists who study the earth, is divided into several sections, each covering an important area of research. A brief description of these areas follows:

Geodesist

Geodesy is the study of the size, shape, and gravitational field of the earth. The principal task of geodesists is the precise measurement of the earth's surface. They use high-flying aircraft and satellites to determine the positions, elevations, and distances between points on the earth.

Geodesists establish observation points all over the earth's surface. This network of points is used for extremely accurate mapping of the elevation of the land above sea level, as well as for the exact location of the point in respect to its latitude and longitude. Geodetic survey maps, which are usually produced by Federal and local government geodesists, are used by farmers, land developers, mining companies, and homeowners to better understand the physical characteristics of the land they own or intend to use.

Gravitational studies of various regions of the earth by geodesists give us insight into the variation in the earth's crust. These measurements can aid in oil exploration and in surveying for such natural resources as iron ore, natural gas, and salt.

Seismologist

Seismology is the study of earthquakes, both natural and man-made. Most of what we know about the interior of the earth has been learned by seismologists studying the behavior of shock waves from large earthquakes and from dynamite explosions set off underground. By studying the shocks from small explosions in the ocean, they have learned about the ocean depths and the structures of the layers below the seafloor.

Seismological studies are used to explore for oil and minerals. Sound waves travel faster through hard rock than through soft coal, and they travel very slowly through liquid pools of oil and gaseous buildups of methane. Therefore, by carefully detonating small explosions in deep wells, these scientists can investigate subsurface land formations quickly and inexpensively.

About 5,000 earthquakes a year occur around the globe. Most are too minor to be felt by any but the most sensitive machines. Seismologists study these quakes to discover ways that might be used to predict when major quakes may happen.

Seismological studies are gaining important recognition through the efforts of groups who point out the hazards involved in locating certain nuclear power plants near faults below the surface. Seismologists also are able to detect underground atomic bomb explosions occurring in foreign countries.

Geomagnetic Physicist and Paleomagnetic Physicist

Geomagnetism or the magnetic field of the earth has been studied for hundreds of years. Christopher Columbus never would have attempted his voyage if it hadn't been for the then recently discovered magnetic compass. However, even today we have only crude explanations for this phenomenon.

The earth's magnetic field originates deep within its core of iron and nickel compressed under millions of tons of pressure, and it extends far into space. It interacts both with magnetic minerals of various rocks and with the magnetic fields of the sun, the moon, and other intergalactic bodies to create the magnetosphere far out in space.

The measurement and study of these interactions require the efforts of many earth scientists. Specialists in this field are called geomagnetic physicists.

The magnetic properties of some kinds of rocks tell scientists how the earth's magnetic field has changed over the last three billion years. These scientists, called paleomagnetic ("paleo-" means old) geophysicists, have discovered that a rock's magnetic field was lined up with the earth's magnetic field when the rock solidified from lava or magma. By studying this "fossil" magnetism, we can learn about shifts in the ocean floor, continental drift, and how the north and south pole have wandered since the planet's creation. Their discoveries are a part of the new field called plate tectonics.

The magnetic field of the earth controls the motion of the earth's ionosphere. This region of electrons and ions is formed by solar X rays and ultraviolet rays colliding with the rarefied gases in the upper atmosphere. Disruptions in the ionosphere affect communication system transmissions and weather and result in the spectacular light emissions called the aurora borealis.

Accurate measurements of the earth's magnetic field continue at a network of geomagnetic stations around the globe. These were first established in 1882. Their results are continuously fed into computers, which plot the earth's ever-changing characteristics.

Volcanologist

Volcanology is the study of volcanoes. It also involves the study of all the forces and processes of the molten, flowing rock that lies only a few miles beneath the surface of any spot on earth. This thermal structure of the earth deposits the ores and forms the rocks that are used by industry. Volcanologists investigate the causes of volcanoes and try to predict when major eruptions may take place. Volcanologists are also trying to find ways of tapping the tremendous subterranean heat for use as an energy resource.

Petrologist

Petrology is the study of the classification and composition of rocks. Some rocks are over three billion years old. How did they form? How do we know how old a rock is? How was the rock made? How are different kinds of rocks distributed over the earth? These are questions the petrologists are trying to solve. The solution to these problems will provide a geochronology, a time scale of geological events, which will help us understand the physical and chemical evolution of the earth.

Geochemist

Geochemists study the chemical composition of the various components of the earth. They are trying to discover the conditions that caused one kind of metal, such as tin, to be deposited in one place while another, such as iron, is found somewhere else. Geochemical studies help mineral and fuel companies to determine the deposits in various areas that might be profitable for development.

Hydrologist

Hydrologists study the occurrence, behavior, and distribution of water in all its forms on and in the earth. The water cycle, evaporation–precipitation–condensation, is the means by which vegetation and annimals, including us, are provided with fresh water, which is becoming increasingly difficult to obtain.

Hydrologists study the watersheds, or freshwater runoff areas, for rivers and streams. If a forest is destroyed by natural or man-made forces, its ability to hold and distribute fresh water may be lost. This erosion can seriously affect the down-river communities that rely on a constant supply. Most fresh water is not flowing above ground, but is found in underground streams, rivers, and rivulets as well as in the soil. This resource must be carefully preserved, and much research is needed to locate and maintain this storage area.

The deltas of Mississippi and Egypt are formed by soil deposited by mighty rivers. This enriched land is used by farmers to provide abundant harvests. Small changes in the flow of the river could bring devastation in the form of drought or flood, which could seriously disrupt the life of the region. More than ten billion dollars a year is spent on hydrologic projects to bring water to cities and crops and to preserve and purify this necessary resource.

Hydrologists also investigate glaciers, ice, snow, and permafrost. They carry out their studies around the globe. Their work is important to agriculture, forestry, biology, and all the other earth sciences.

Technophysicist

Technophysics is one of the newest branches of geophysics. It involves a study of how the earth's crust has moved and changed since it solidified from cosmic material about five billion years ago. The seafloor is spreading, causing down-warping trenches that are the deepest recesses in the earth. A generally accepted theory that a huge single continent split up millions of years ago, creating today's seven continents, is being studied by technophysicists. They are investigating fossil and rock formations that are similar in both western Africa and eastern Brazil, which are shaped like two jigsaw puzzle pieces that can easily be fitted together. Technophysicists are trying to discover the forces that produce these changes and their effects on volcanology and seismology. The San Andreas fault in California may be caused by these continental shifts, and an understanding of the principles involved can provide methods for easing the pressures slowly, so that a major earthquake may be avoided.

Exploration Geophysicist

Exploration geophysicists are the scientists who find the geological conditions that might indicate valuable oil, natural gas, or mineral deposits below the surface. They do not drill the wells, nor dig into the earth; instead they carefully study and survey an area with gravimeters, magnetometers, portable seismographs, and other delicate equipment and predict whether the area is worth further investigation.

Nearly one billion dollars a year is spent on geophysical exploration for new oil reserves. In addition, the exploration geophysicists search for radioactive ores for atomic energy, as well as new deposits of iron ore, copper, tin, zinc, and other metals.

Where Geophysicists Work

Most geophysicists work in private industry, chiefly for petroleum and natural gas companies. Other work for mining companies, exploration and consulting firms, and research institutes. A few are independent consultants, and some do geophysical prospecting on a fee or contract basis.

Geophysicists are employed in many Southwestern and Western states and in those on the Gulf Coast, where large oil and natural gas fields are located.

Many geophysicists work in offices in large metropolitan regions, where they use computers to help them analyze the data sent from all regions of the globe and from outer space. Some geophysicists work in laboratories, where they analyze samples to learn their composition. Some laboratories try to recreate the conditions that cause geologic changes so that the scientists can find ways to predict where oil fields might be, how earthquakes damage buildings, how water is stored in various kinds of soils, and so on. Computer simulation is a new and powerful technique for carrying out "experiments" with the earth that could never actually be performed.

Most geophysicists, at some point in their career or training, carry out field work, which may be in any portion of the world, on land, at sea, in the air, or, for some, in outer space. Often the choice of the area rests with the scientist. Many request foreign work where they can explore deserts, jungles, and mountains as well as visit exotic cities.

Almost 25 percent of all geophysicists work for the Federal government. Many are assigned to jobs in and around Washington, D.C., and in Denver, Colorado, where the National Oceanic and Atmospheric Administration has a large headquarters. The U.S. Geological Survey has offices around the U.S., and geophysicists work for the Defense Department at bases around the globe. Other geophysicists work for colleges and universities, state governments, and nonprofit research institutions.

Geophysicists usually begin their careers as trainees after graduating from college. Trainees learn to handle the sophisticated electronic equipment used by geophysicists. They learn to record data, feed it into the computers, and interpret the results. Trainees work in the field and become familiar with all phases of the operation. This on-the-job training enhances the skills the scientist learned at college and teaches him or her the special requirements of the firm that is paying for the job.

How You Can Train for a Job in Geophysics

A bachelor's degree with a major in geophysics or a geophysical specialty is the usual requirement for beginning jobs in the field. About 50 colleges and universities award the bachelor's degree in geophysics. Other colleges, although not specifically offering geophysics degrees, give bachelor's degrees in such fields as geophysical engineering, petroleum geology, and geodesy. Many colleges offer programs in earth science or geology that many prepare a student for a career in geophysics.

Some beginning jobs in geophysics are available for people with bachelor's degrees in related disciplines such as chemistry, physics, engineering, or mathematics, who also have taken coursework, or minored, in geophysics.

Research and supervisory jobs in geophysics usually require graduate training. A master's degree or a doctorate is often a prerequisite for any high-level job. About 60 universities grant graduate degrees in geophysics. Often a person who studies geophysics in graduate school may have an undergraduate degree in another branch of the sciences or in mathematics.

If you want to become a geophysicist, you should take a strong college-preparatory program in high school. You will need biology, chemistry, and physics. If your school offers earth science, astronomy, or oceanography, you should take these courses, too, but only in addition to the biology, chemistry, and physics. You will need a lot of mathematics in geophysics. Take intermediate algebra, trigonometry, and geometry. If you can take a course in calculus, that will help. Certainly, take a course in computer science, if available.

English and social studies courses will prepare you with the communications skills and historical background you will need to be an effective scientist. Geophysicists often travel and work in countries around the world; therefore, a knowledge of one or more modern foreign languages is very helpful.

In college the geophysics major usually takes calculus, physics, chemistry, and introductory geophysics courses during his first two years, along with coursework in English composition, foreign languages, psychology, economics, and so on. In his or her junior and senior year, the coursework will be specialized and may include geochemistry, geophysical methods, electromagnetism, engineering, and so on.

In graduate school the geophysics major will take courses in his or her particular field of interest such as seismology, volcanology, hydrology, geodesy. For a PhD, the student must do an original research project in geophysics, and prepare a dissertation. This work is sponsored by a committee of professors who are experts in their field.

Many geophysicists enter the field with a bachelor's degree and attend graduate school part time. Often this training is paid for by the company for which the scientist works.

Opportunities for Geophysicists

The employment outlook for graduates in the field of geophysics is excellent. The energy crisis has created a need in this very specialized field. The Federal government in the mid-1970's predicted that there would be about 800 openings a year for geophysicists. However, the need has significantly increased.

It is very important to realize that few qualified people enter the field each year. Fewer than 200 graduates a year are trained in geophysics. It is an occupation requiring a very special set of interests and skills, and many people are neither qualified nor adept at developing these abilities.

Employment in geophysics will grow much faster than the average for all occupations in the 1980's. As known deposits of petroleum and other minerals are depleted, petroleum and mining companies will need increasing numbers of geophysicists who can use sophisticated electronic techniques to find less accessible fuel and mineral deposits.

In addition, geophysicists with advanced training will be needed to do research on radioactivity, cosmic and solar radiation, geothermal (heat from inside the earth) and tidal power, and so on to find new resources of energy for generating electricity.

The Federal government and private industry are preparing to spend billions of dollars to aid research in fields that need geophysicists, and hundreds of new jobs should be opening in this important occupation.

Geophysicists with bachelor's degrees had an average starting salary of $23,500 in 1982, those with master's degrees could start at $28,000. and those with doctorates at approximately $34,000. The average salary for geophysicists in 1982 was $35,200.

Where You Can Obtain Training in Geophysics

Some of the colleges and universities that offer a major in geophysics are:

University of Alabama, Birmingham, Alabama 35294
Baylor University, Waco, Texas 76703
Bowling Green State University, Bowling Green, Ohio 43403
University of Chicago, Chicago, Illinois 60637
Colgate University, Hamilton, New York 13346
Colorado School of Mines, Golden, Colorado 80401
De Pauw University, Greencastle, Indiana 46135
Duquesne University, Pittsburgh, Pennsylvania 15219
Harvard University, Cambridge, Massachusetts 02138
University of Houston, Houston, Texas 77004
Johns Hopkins University, Baltimore, Maryland 21218
Louisiana Technical University, Ruston, Louisiana 71270
Michigan State University, East Lansing, Michigan 48824
Michigan Tech University, Houghton, Michigan 49931
Northwestern University, Evanston, Illinois 60201
Pennsylvania State University, University Park, Pennsylvania 16802
Purdue University, Fort Wayne, Indiana 46805
Rice University, Houston, Texas 77001
St. Lawrence University, Canton, New York 13617
Stanford University, Stanford, California 94305
State University of New York, Stony Brook, New York 11790
Stevens Institute of Technology, Hoboken, New Jersey 07030
Texas A & M University, College Station, Texas 77843
Tulane University, New Orleans, Louisiana 70118
University of Tulsa, Tulsa, Oklahoma 74104
Virginia Polytechnical Institute, Blacksburg, Virginia 24061
Wesleyan University, Middletown, Connecticut 06457
Wittenberg University, Springfield, Ohio 45501

More Information on Geophysics Careers

For more information, write to:

Society of Exploration Geophysicists
P.O. Box 3098
Tulsa, OK 74101

American Geophysical Union
1909 K Street, NW
Washington, DC 20006

For more information about jobs in the Federal government, write to:

U.S. Civil Service Commission
1900 E Street, NW
Washington, DC 20250

For detailed information about the field read:

Your Future in Geology by Joseph L. Weitz, Richards Rosen Press.

C. CAREERS IN METEOROLOGY

Meteorology is the study of the atmosphere and the weather. Meteorologists observe weather conditions around the globe, try to understand what caused their development, and try to predict what the weather is going to do next. Meteorology involves the use of chemistry, physics, mathematics, geology, oceanography, and other sciences.

As you probably know, the suffix "ology" means "study of." The prefix "meteor" means heavenly or celestial. Historically, meteorology was a study of the sky, and we know today that our weather is directly influenced by the major object in the sky, our sun. The sun supplies the energy for the water cycle, which continuously produces evaporation of water from the oceans, rain over the land, and the watershedding of streams and rivers across the land. The sun and the moon produce the gravitational pulls that attract the oceans' tides. The heating of the atmosphere produces the high- and low-pressure areas that cause the wind patterns, which in turn blow the clouds over the earth and the waves upon the seas.

The study of weather, as you can see, is very complex. A great deal of physics is involved in explaining and interpreting the causes and movements of weather fronts. Chemistry is needed for interpreting the crystallizing forces within a cloud, or the effects of pollutants on the atmosphere. And, of course, mathematics and computer science are of utmost value to the meteorologist.

Meteorologists perform different tasks on different jobs. The biggest employer of meteorologists is the National Weather Service, which is part of the National Oceanic and Atmospheric Administration (NOAA) of the U.S. Department of Commerce. Meteorologists at the Weather

Service constantly observe the weather and continuously record the temperature, humidity, barometric pressure, wind velocity, pollutants, spores (for hay fever sufferers), and other variables in the air. These meteorologists may work in office buildings in major cities; in laboratories on remote islands, deserts, or mountain ranges; on ships cruising the oceans; at airports; or in aircraft flying throughout the troposphere and the lower stratosphere. The conditions of the upper stratosphere are studied by scientists with weather balloons and rockets.

Satellites, such as the TIROS and NIMBUS, send global weather data to U.S. tracking stations positioned around the world. On the six o'clock news we can see satellite weather photographs of huge storm fronts moving across the continental United States.

The data collected from these weather observers are sent to weather analysts and forecasters at centrally located bureaus. These highly skilled specialists chart the isolated data on weather maps and feed the information into high-speed computers. It is their job to predict what the weather will be like for your home town, for farmers, for pilots, for sea captains, for sporting events, and so on.

Weather forecasters and observers are on the job around the clock, every day of the year. They must have a careful and inquiring mind and the desire to do the best possible job. They must be especially reliable. Their reports often go unchecked, and the information may be responsible for the lives of many people. For example, careless weather observations have led to airplane accidents.

Meteorologists who specialize in forecasting the weather are known professionally as synoptic meteorologists. They are the largest group of specialists.

Physical Meteorologist

Physical meteorologists study the chemical and electrical properties of the atmosphere. They do research on the effect of the atmosphere on transmission of light, sound, and radio waves. They investigate the factors that form clouds, hurricanes, and rain. They are concerned with the effect of pollutants, such as fluorochlorocarbons from aerosol sprays, on the upper atmosphere. This pollutant causes the ozone, which absorbs dangerous ultraviolet radiation from the sun, to break down into regular oxygen, which cannot protect us from this radiation. They are also concerned with factory and car emissions that combine with rain to form acids, which fall on our crops, wildlife, and cities. "Acid rains" and gaseous pollutants have enveloped the earth and have been found in the most remote regions of the arctic wastelands.

Climatologist

Climatologists are meteorologists who study climatic trends and analyze historical records on wind, rainfall, sunshine, and temperature to determine the general patterns of weather that have occurred over an area for an extended period of time. Climate is the average weather condition over several years (or even several centuries). Before city planners, major builders, or agricultural conglomerates begin a costly project, they want to know how much rain an area normally gets, how the temperature varies, whether the area is subject to tornadoes or floods, and so on. Climatologists are trying to discover the prehistoric conditions that led to a tropical forest over what is now New Jersey, and to the ice ages that covered Europe and most of North America with continental glaciers. They are investigating whether the earth is getting warmer annually, or colder. And they are concerned with the effects on the earth's climate of smoke and carbon dioxide from hydrocarbon exhausts.

Air Pollution Meteorologist

Meteorologists who specialize in air pollution are making important contributions to an understanding of how pollutants are carried, spread, and accumulated in high concentrations in the atmosphere. Their expertise is needed to warn the public of possible changes in pollution levels. In order to improve the methods for predicting air quality, air pollution meteorologists analyze the relationships between weather and pollution using statistical methods.

Using information from the National Weather Service and local measurements of pollutant concentrations, control agencies are able to protect the public by enforcing restrictions to eliminate, or at least reduce, pollutants in the atmosphere. Emergency actions may include reducing the operation of power plants, reducing or shutting down the operations of industry, and closing highways to traffic.

Meteorologists on an air-quality team are expected to advise other scientists and engineers on problems involving weather or climate. They recommend sites for air-quality measuring instruments. They advise on the best locations for power plants or industrial parks and help in preparing environmental impact statements, predicting how proposed projects will affect air quality.

Other Meteorologists

Other meteorologists apply their training to specific problems. Some work in aerospace engineering, where they aid in the design of aircraft and spacecraft. Some specialize in agriculture, where they help farmers adapt their crops and methods to changing weather patterns. Droughts and storms have ruined millions of acres of farmland over the last few decades, and agricultural meteorologists are trying to understand these conditions and find ways to prevent or, at least, cope with them.

Biometeorologists study the effects of the atmosphere on living things. They are interested in how weather changes cause physiological and psychological changes in man and other species. Some biometeorologists have theories that connect air pressure abnormalities with general feelings of anxiety and uneasiness among a population. In other words, they think that on days when "everybody" seems irritable, there might be a weather or pollution factor influencing a city. Others have found that certain animal species react differently days before a hurricane approaches, although the general weather conditions appear unaffected.

Civil engineers work with specially trained meteorologists in designing buildings, piers, beachfronts, dams, and so on that can withstand prevalent weather conditions. Electrical engineers and communications specialists also work with meteorologists who are familiar with how the atmosphere affects radio waves, radar, and television signals.

Paleoclimatology is the study of early climates. Geologists working with these scientists may be able to find oil and natural gas fields, since these fuels were formed from tropical forests that were heaved underground millions of years ago.

Meteorologists also work for broadcasting stations and news media. Their weather reports are seen by millions, who plan their picnics, parades, trips, and clothing on the forecasts. Sometimes actors or models merely present the reports from the National Weather Service. But more often the personalities are highly trained meteorologists who try to interpret the weather conditions for the public, and stress the ever-changing factors that can cause a prediction for a sunny day to end up as a six-hour thunderstorm.

About one-third of all civilian meteorologists work primarily in weather forecasting and measurement, and another one-third work in research and development. About one-fifth of all civilians in this occupation work as administrators and in management positions.

Some meteorologists teach and do research in colleges and universities. Some teach earth science in secondary school systems. In institutions without separate meteorology or earth science departments, they may teach geography, mathematics, physics, chemistry, or geology as well as meteorology.

Where Meteorologists Work

In 1980 only about 6,000 meteorologists were employed in the United States. In addition to these civilian meteorologists, thousands of members of the Army, Navy, Air Force, and Coast Guard did forecasting and other meteorological work.

The largest employer of civilian meteorologists was the National Oceanic and Atmospheric Administration. Over 2,100 scientists worked at stations in all parts of the U.S. and in a small number of foreign countries in 1978. The Department of Defense employed over 200 meteorologists.

Other meteorologists who worked for the Federal government worked at the Department of Energy, the National Aeronautics and Space Administration, the Federal Aviation Administration, the Department of Agriculture, and the Department of Health and Human Services.

Almost 2,000 meteorologists worked for private enterprise. Commercial airlines employed several hundred to forecast weather along flight routes and to brief pilots on weather conditions. Others worked for the aerospace industry aiding in the design of aircraft and space vehicles that would fly through the atmosphere and its weather. They worked for communications and broadcasting companies, helping them send better signals and reporting the weather. Transportation companies and energy corporations need meteorologists to help with the routing of shipments and energy resources. Merchants and the food industry rely on their own meteorologists to supply accurate, pertinent information for protecting the shipment of perishable goods and for planting and harvesting produce. Also, some meteorologists work as private consultants and for private research organizations.

Beginning meteorologists often start in jobs involving routine data collection, computation, or analysis. Experienced meteorologists may advance to supervisory or administrative jobs. A few well-qualified meteorologists with a background in science, engineering, and business administration may establish their own weather consulting services.

How You Can Train for a Job in Meteorology

A bachelor's degree with a major in meteorology is the usual minimum requirement for beginning jobs in weather forecasting. However, a bachelor's degree in a related science or engineering, along with some courses in meteorology, is acceptable for some jobs. For example, the Federal government's minimum requirement for beginning jobs is a bachelor's degree with at least 20 semester hours of study in meteorology and courses in physics and mathematics, including calculus. However, employers prefer to hire those with an advanced degree, and an advanced degree is increasingly necessary for advancement.

When you are in high school, you should take a well-balanced college preparatory program. Mathematics is the principal tool of the meteorologist. You should study as much of it as possible. Intermediate algebra is essential. To succeed in meteorology, you should find mathematics relatively interesting and not too hard. Geometry and trigonometry courses will help you prepare for your career. Computer training, if available, will be very helpful.

Since meteorology involves international cooperation, knowledge of French, German, Russian, or Chinese will help you considerably. A candidate with ability in one of these languages will have a much better chance of obtaining a job.

English is, of course, absolutely necessary. You must be able to communicate accurately and easily in both writing and speaking. You should be able to describe events logically, clearly, and completely.

The prediction of weather involves a thorough knowledge of chemistry and physics of the atmosphere and its interaction with land and sea. In high school you should study both chemistry and physics. If earth science is offered, use it as an additional elective, but do not substitute it for either chemistry or physics. Biology is necessary for understanding the ecological and natural influences of weather.

In college you have to decide if you want to major in meteorology or major in another science field with meteorology as your minor. In 1978 there were more than 50 universities and colleges in the U.S. and Canada offering the bachelor's degree in meteorology. The principal advantage in majoring in meteorology as an undergraduate is that you may go to work as a meteorologist directly upon graduation. You will be able to begin a career, but you will probably lack enough training in physics, chemistry, and advanced mathematics to engage in any research.

To prepare for a research specialization, you may continue your education at the graduate level, or you may study advanced physics or mathematics in college while taking meteorological coursework. A number of interesting and valuable interdisciplinary careers become accessible if you combine a degree in meteorology with a degree in another major subject. Joint degrees with meteorology have been awarded in aerospace engineering, agriculture, astronomy, biology, civil and environmental engineering, electrical engineering, geology, journalism, communications, mathematics, and oceanography. People with these backgrounds can expect interesting jobs and have allowed themselves the opportunity to change occupations or select new careers as they move up the career ladder or as opportunities afford themselves.

Meteorology training has been effectively combined with law, medicine, speech, and business administration. Physics and chemistry have proved to be the most fruitful of all the interdisciplinary areas. Scientists with extensive training in these fields have contributed to major advances in our understanding of the atmosphere. The meteorological satellites and the man-in-space program are outstanding examples of career activities involving various aspects of science and engineering.

Some respected research meteorologists and teachers think that it may be best not to major in meteorology until graduate school. They feel that rigorous training in the traditional sciences and mathematics is the best preparation for today's jobs in weather forecasting.

Advanced work requires a master's degree or doctorate. More than fifty-five colleges in the United States and Canada offer graduate work through the doctorate in meteorology and closely allied fields. Doctoral work requires difficult, advanced training and an original research project that will culminate in a dissertation on your contribution to the understanding of the atmosphere. Many meteorologists study for their graduate degrees under work-study or part-time arrangements with their employers.

A excellent way to receive training in meteorology is through the armed services. The U.S. Army, Air Force, and Navy have extensive meteorological facilities staffed by persons whom they have trained. These services offer special programs often in affiliation with degree-granting universities, where you can obtain meteorological skills and a degree while serving your tour of duty.

Opportunities for Meteorologists
There should be about 200 openings a year for meteorologists. Although the number of new jobs created by growth in the occupation and the openings due to replacement needs is relatively small, the number of persons obtaining degrees in meteorology also is small. If trends in the number of degrees granted continue, the number of people seeking entry to the field will about equal the requirements.

Employment in the field is expected to increase about 15 to 25 percent over the next ten years. Jobs in industry and in weather consulting firms are expected to grow as these concerns discover how people trained in meteorology can help them meet clean air standards and increase production.

The aviation industry and the aerospace projects may need additional meteorologists as their importance grows in the 1980's. There should also be some openings in radio and television as local stations are finding that trained meteorologists present better weather reporting than actors who must rely on weather service reports that may be several hours behind a developing weather situation.

Colleges and universities will offer some job opportunities, but only for those meteorologists with advanced degrees. Secondary schools, too, should have some new jobs as earth science and environmental science become more popular. Jobs in the secondary schools will require some specialized training in teaching. Also, as in the community college, and perhaps in the university, meteorological faculty may well be expected to teach courses in physics, mathematics, and other allied fields.

The employment of civilian meteorologists in the Federal government is not expected to grow significantly in the next decade, although there will be openings created by replacement needs. The National Weather Service hired few professional-level meteorologists in 1983; instead, it hired meteorological technicians, most at a starting salary of $13,369. The average salary for all meteorologists in 1982 was $34,200. For beginning professionals, those with bachelor's degrees averaged $16,000, those with master's degrees $20,000, and those with doctorates $26,000.

Where You Can Obtain Training in Meteorology
Some of the colleges and universities that offer a major in meteorology are:

Colorado State University, Fort Collins, Colorado 80523
Columbia University, New York, New York 10027
Drexel University, Philadelphia, Pennsylvania 19104
Florida State University, Tallahassee, Florida 32306
Georgia Institute of Technology, Atlanta, Georgia 30332
Harvard University, Cambridge, Massachusetts 02138
Johns Hopkins University, Baltimore, Maryland 21218
Massachusetts Institute of Technology, Cambridge, Massachusetts 02139
McGill University, Quebec, Canada H3C 3G1
Montana State University, Bozeman, Montana 59717
New Mexico Institute of Mining and Technology, Socorro, New Mexico 87801
Ohio State University, Columbus, Ohio 43210
Oregon State University, Corvallis, Oregon 97331
Pennsylvania State University—University Park Campus, University Park, Pennsylvania 16802
Princeton University, Princeton, New Jersey 08544
Rice University, Houston, Texas 77001
Rutgers University, New Brunswick, New Jersey 08903
Saint Louis University, St. Louis, Missouri 63108
San Jose State University, San Jose, California 95912
South Dakota School of Mines and Technology, Rapid City, South Dakota 57701
Stanford University, Stanford, California 94305
State University of New York at Albany, Albany, New York 12222
State University of New York at Stony Brook, Stony Brook, New York 11794
Texas A & M University, College Station, Texas 77843
Trenton State College, Trenton, New Jersey 08625
University of Alaska, Fairbanks, Alaska 99701

University of Alberta, Edmonton, Alberta, Canada T6G 2G1
University of Arizona, Tucson, Arizona 85721
University of California, Berkeley, Berkeley, California 94720
University of California, San Diego, San Diego, California 92093
University of Chicago, Chicago, Illinois 60637
University of Colorado, Boulder, Colorado 80309
University of Florida, Gainesville, Florida 32611
University of Hawaii at Monoa, Honolulu, Hawaii 96822
University of Maryland at College Park, College Park, Maryland 20742
University of Miami, Coral Gables, Florida 33124
University of Michigan, Ann Arbor, Michigan 48109
University of Missouri—Columbia, Columbia, Missouri 65211
University of Nevada, Las Vegas, Nevada 89154
University of Oklahoma, Norman, Oklahoma 73019
University of Texas at El Paso, El Paso, Texas 79968
University of Utah, Salt Lake City, Utah 84112
University of Washington, Seattle, Washington 98195
University of Wisconsin—Madison, Madison, Wisconsin 53706
University of Wyoming, Laramie, Wyoming 82071

More Information on Meteorology Centers
To obtain further information, write to:

American Meteorological Society
45 Beacon Street
Boston, MA 02108

American Geophysical Union
1909 K Street, NW
Washington, DC 20006

For information about careers in the Federal government write to:

U.S. Civil Service Commission
1900 E Street, NW
Washington, DC 20250

National Oceanic and Atmospheric Administration
6001 Executive Boulevard
Rockville, MD 20852

D. CAREERS IN OCEANOGRAPHY

The world is really one huge ocean, broken here and there by islands that we call continents. To an outer space observer, our planet is blue. Its name should be, perhaps, Oceanus, instead of earth. The oceans cover over 140 million square miles of the earth's surface and reach depths of more than six miles. All of the 92 natural elements can be found in seawater, including millions of tons of gold and silver. The ocean is filled with life. Plants grow along the shore and on the ocean's surface. An amazing variety of animals, some microscopic and some weighing several tons, are found in the sea. Some of the animals float on the surface, some swim, and others live on the seafloor. The ocean is never still. Its shoreline is constantly shifting, and its surface is forever being ripped by waves. Currents flow beneath its surface, bringing warm waters to Europe and cold, enriched nutrients to the fishing banks off Labrador.

COURTESY PHILLIPS PETROLEUM COMPANY
Oceanographers assist petroleum engineers in the construction of
oil platforms at sea.

Oceanography is the study of the sea. Oceanographers are attempting to understand and explain the processes within the ocean; and the interrelationship between the ocean and the land, and the ocean and the atmosphere. Oceanography involves the animals and plants that inhabit the oceans, the minerals and fuels deposited within the seafloor, the weather formed when the atmosphere meets the sea, the shoreline, the tides, the beaches, the waves, and the sea currents. Oceanographic research involves geology, meteorology, biology, chemistry, physics, geophysics, geochemistry, fluid mechanics, and mathematics.

Many phases of marine research can be studied in the laboratory, but to truly understand the ocean scientists must frequently go to sea in specially constructed and equipped research ships. Sometimes data regarding the shoreline, the beach, and the tides are obtained by oceanographers in a small dinghy; often, larger ships cruise the seas for months with a crew of several oceanographers; and sometimes these scientists go below the surface in scuba gear, diving suits, submarines, and, to reach the deepest regions, in bathyspheres.

The projects of oceanographers help in developing more accurate weather forecasts, breeding more fish for food, finding oil and minerals for economic and industrial growth, and aiding in the national defense. In recent years, the dangers of pollution from underwater mining of gas and oil, tanker oil spills, and industrial waste have led the public to look toward the oceanographer for ways to safeguard our water.

Twenty-nine percent of the American population lives along the coast where industries spill their wastewater into the ocean. In addition, urban sewer systems carry domestic wastes, sometimes treated and sometimes not, into the sea. The oceanographer must study the effect of these pollutants on the ocean and advise the sanitary engineer as to what corrective action is needed. At the same time, oceanographers are also exploring the ocean for new freshwater sources.

Some oceanographers work in laboratories associated with universities, where they study the minute details of animal and plant life found in the oceans. They may measure, dissect, and photograph fish. They may examine under high-powered microscopes the plankton, tiny plants and animals that float on the surface of the oceans and serve as the major food source for most fish and sea animals, including the mammoth whales. These scientists are intrigued by identifying, cataloguing, and minutely observing the characteristics of the sea's living organisms.

Other oceanographers are interested in the mineral wealth of the seafloor. Using ultrasonic sonar, they probe the depths to locate likely regions where the sea has covered regions of prehistoric forests that have now turned to oil and natural gas. They map mountain ranges grander than the Rockies and gorges far deeper and wider than the Grand Canyon. If a possible resource is discovered, the oceanographer may suggest that extremely expensive drilling or mining begin.

Oceanographers explore and study the ocean from the surface, the beach, underwater, and from the air. The latest explorations are being carried out from satellites. They are charting the currents, the ocean depths, the temperature gradients, and the weather formed where the sea and atmosphere meet.

Oceanographers use specialized instruments to measure and record the findings of their explorations and studies. Special cameras equipped with strong lights are used to photograph marine life and the seafloor. Underwater seismometers record the echoes from underwater earthquakes and from depth charges ignited by scientists. Sonar units are used to detect schools of fish, underwater land formations, and submarines.

Oceanographers want to know everything they can about the sea. They measure the salt content, which changes at various levels and in different bodies of water. They check on wave heights and the speed of currents. They want to know each and every kind of living species that inhabits the sea, and they want to understand the environmental factors that allow these plants and creatures survival.

Many phases of oceanography overlap, but a few occupations can be distinguished.

Physical Oceanographer

Physical oceanographers study ocean currents, waves and tides, the chemical composition of seawater, and the sediments that fall to the bottom. Physical oceanographers work with meteorologists and geophysicists in trying to understand the processes of nature.

Chemical Oceanographer

Chemical oceanographers investigate the chemical processes of the sea. The difference in salinity, salt content, between the Mediterranean Sea and the Atlantic Ocean allowed German U-boat commanders to slip past the sonar installations at Gibraltar by turning off their engines and allowing the osmotic force to propel them. Different kinds of marine life require different salt contents for survival, as well as different amounts of dissolved oxygen in the water. Undersea mining, oil wells, and global pollution have greatly affected the chemical content of seawater, which may cause the extinction of many species.

Geological Oceanographer

Geological oceanography is the study of the geological processes in the seafloor and along the shores. These marine geologists study the ocean's underwater mountain ranges, rocks, and sediments. Most are employed in trying to locate regions where oil, minerals, and natural gas might be found under the seafloor. One group of these scientists are working with plate tectonic geophysicists in studying and testing the theory of continental shift.

Biological Oceanographer

Biological oceanography is the study of the living creatures of the ocean. These scientists investigate the ecology, physiology, and taxonomy of plants and creatures of the sea. Many marine biologists specialize in one group of creatures, such as sharks, mollusks, or sea worms. Some are working with agronomists to produce sea vegetation that can be harvested for human consumption. Others are trying to improve and control commercial fishing and to determine the effects of pollution on marine life.

Fishery

Fishery is an applied branch of marine biology, which includes the problems of marketing, storing, and preparation of food fish. It is concerned with the biology of fishes, their population control, the changes that currents, tides, overfishing, and pollution have on the market value of fish. The industry is sometimes called aquaculture.

Where Oceanographers Work

Only about 3,000 persons were working as oceanographers in 1980. It is one of the smallest of all scientific fields. This is rather surprising, considering the vastness and value of the oceans. However, neither the Federal government nor private industry wants to invest the capital required to develop the basic scientific understandings that will lead to a utilization of this resource.

About one-half of all oceanographers work as research and teaching faculty at colleges and universities. These professors spend about 50 percent of their time working with students, and the rest carrying out their investigations. Most of the universities that employ oceanographers are, of course, on either the Atlantic or Pacific coast. A few, however, are inland.

The Federal government employs about one-fourth of all oceanographers. Many work for the National Oceanic and Atmospheric Administration or the Department of the Navy. The National Ocean Survey prepares charts and tables for navigation, for fishing, and for hydrographic studies. It has a fleet of research and survey ships that chart the coastal waters and tides.

The National Weather Service uses oceanographers to study the interaction between the atmosphere and the oceans, and to report on weather conditions at sea. The Environmental Research Laboratories of NOAA are carrying out basic research on the coastal environment, oceanic processes, the forces that produce severe storms and tsunamis, and so on. The National Fisheries Service seeks to develop the fishing industry in coastal waters and to protect the habitat of commercial and sport fish.

Some oceanographers work in private industry. They work for large shipping companies, for aquaculture corporations, and for mining and oil companies seeking fuel and minerals beneath the sea. State and local aquaria groups and a few private foundations, such as the International Oceanographic Foundation and The Cousteau Society, employ oceanographers to carry out basic research and to publicize and popularize the sea's important function in our global survival.

Most oceanographers work in states that border on the ocean, although there are some oceanographers in every state. Four out of ten oceanographers work in just three states—California, Maryland, and Virginia.

Oceanographers, whatever their special interest, are really sailor-scientists. They must go to sea for their information. Therefore, if you want to be an oceanographer, you should enjoy a life at sea. This may include days or weeks of tedious boredom, bad storms, repetitious recording of detailed data, seasickness, and long absences from the mainland. Many oceanographers are gathering information by making deep-sea dives in bathyspheres, submarines, and diving suits. Others use scuba outfits to investigate the water within 40 feet of the surface. Once the data is obtained, the oceanographers may spend months and years analyzing their findings at laboratories and computer centers back home.

How You Can Train for a Job in Oceanography

The minimum requirement for beginning professional jobs in oceanography is a bachelor's degree in oceanography, biology, geology, mathematics, or chemistry. However, most jobs in oceanography require graduate training, and a doctoral degree is often preferred or required. There are very few openings for oceanographers, so the competition is keen. Only the most capable scientists will find jobs.

Oceanographers must be expert in mathematics, physics, geology, biology, and chemistry. To understand the oceans, the marine scientist must work with all the relationships in nature's physical-biological world. A biological oceanographer studying the habitat of a species of fish must investigate the chemistry of the seawater, the geology of the seafloor, the pressure exerted by the water above, the speed of the currents, the nature of the wave action, the temperature and light variations, as well as the anatomical structure of the creature, its activities, its sociology, its prey, and its predators.

In high school a future oceanographer must take chemistry, physics, and biology as well as any other science courses available. Oceanography is sometimes offered in secondary schools as an elective. Of course, this would be a good course, but do not take it instead of the major disciplines. Use it, along with subjects like photography and earth science, as extra preparation.

High school students who want to be oceanographers must obtain a solid background in mathematics. Take intermediate algebra, geometry, and trigonometry. If calculus is offered, it will make your advanced studies easier. Computer science is important in all fields of science; if a course is available at your school, you should take it, too.

Good English is essential. An oceanographer must be able to skillfully report his research to other scientists. You must be competent in English composition, have good sentence structure, and be able to express your ideas clearly and logically.

Jacques Cousteau, the most famous oceanographer, combined his interest in marine science and history to discover antiquities and sunken treasure ships at the bottom of the sea.

Since the oceans surround the globe and are vital for the commerce and defense of all nations of the world, the study of foreign languages is very useful to the oceanographer. French, Russian, Chinese, and Spanish are helpful and should be studied for two or more years in high school.

Only about thirty-five colleges offered undergraduate degrees in oceanography or marine science in 1976. However, a future oceanographer can receive a bachelor's degree in mathematics, physics, chemistry, geophysics, geology, meteorology, or biology and still anticipate acceptance in a graduate program in marine science. In fact, many graduate schools would prefer teaching the chemistry of seawater to a chemist, rather than trying to teach analytic chemistry to an oceanographer.

College students planning for careers in the marine sciences should acquire a strong undergraduate major in the basic sciences. The student should take courses in chemistry, physics, earth science or geology, and biology. Mathematics through calculus, statistics, and computer training are usually required for acceptance to a graduate program. Engineering courses and training in meteorology are very helpful. Of course, if you can major in oceanography as an undergraduate, that's teriffic. However, make sure that you minor in one of the other sciences, so that you will have a broad background.

If your college does not offer coursework in oceanography, you may want to take introductory summer courses in marine science at a marine laboratory associated with a major university. Summer programs are offered at the University of Miami, Duke University, the University of Texas, Florida State University, Fairleigh Dickinson University, and the Marine Biological Laboratory at Woods Hole, Massachusetts.

In 1976 over sixty-five colleges offered graduate degrees in oceanography and marine sciences. Nineteen schools offer PhD degrees. The doctorate is required for most high-level research in the field. In graduate school the student receives advanced coursework. He or she trains under experts in the various specialized fields of oceanography. The student will often spend several months at sea, learning the techniques of the marine scientist. Only those who have very good academic credentials will be accepted to graduate programs in oceanography.

For the doctorate the candidate must write a dissertation on original research in oceanography. The doctoral student usually has to have mastered one or two foreign languages, as well as advanced mathematics, the physical and natural sciences, statistics, and computer programming.

The graduate program you might pick will depend on the areas of specialization that each school teaches. Some colleges specialize in fishery science or physical oceanography, whereas others offer broader ranges of studies.

Opportunities for Oceanographers

There will be only about 150 new jobs in oceanography every year. Most oceanographers are not near the age of retirement, so it is expected that there will be very few job openings, and the people hired will have exceptional credentials. Those with a PhD degree should have a more favorable chance of finding employment in this field than others.

The jobs for oceanographers will be found at aquatic research stations, at state and Federal organizations, in industry, and at the science departments of universities and colleges. Many of the jobs are financed by grants from the Federal government; therefore if the government or industry discovers the value of marine research, the job market may mushroom.

A few current projects that might increase the need for oceanographers are:

a) the mining of minerals, including iodine, magnesium, bromine, manganese, nickel, copper, and cobalt, from the sea.

b) the finding of oil and natural gas deposits in areas where drilling is profitable.

c) the harvesting of fish and seaweeds more profitably. Seaweed, incidentally, is now used in making medicine, candy, ice cream, jelly, salad dressing, and cosmetics.

d) the inexpensive desalting of seawater to make it fresh, so that it can be used as an irrigant and a water supply in desert countries.

e) the harnessing of the sea's energy to provide electricity.

f) the development of an inexpensive method for producing hydrogen from seawater. Hydrogen is an almost perfect fuel, whose waste product is water.

g) a global commitment to the elimination of pollution from the sea. As the world's population increases, it will need more and more resources, including food, from the oceans. If the sea continues to be a dumping ground for sewage and industrial, chemical, and radioactive wastes, mankind's life on earth is extremely limited.

These are a few areas in which rapid development could encourage the hiring of more trained oceanographers. However, you must be aware that each year many young people with training in marine science fail to find jobs. Those who get the jobs often have combined an interest in oceanography with experience and training in another scientific field or with engineering.

Oceanographers receive relatively high salaries. Those with bachelor's degrees start at $16,000, those with master's degrees at $20,000, and those with doctorates at $28,000. The average salary of experienced oceanographers in 1982 was nearly $32,000.

Where You Can Obtain Training in Oceanography

Some of the colleges and universities that offer a major in oceanography are:

Alfred University, Alfred, New York 14802
Boston University, Boston, Massachusetts 02167
Bowdoin College, Brunswick, Maine 04011
University of Bridgeport, Bridgeport, Connecticut 06602
Catholic University, Washington, D.C. 20017
Clark University, Worcester, Massachusetts 01610
Columbia University, New York, N.Y. 10027
University of Connecticut, Storrs, Connecticut 06268
University of Delaware, Newark, Delaware 19711
Duke University, Durham, North Carolina 27706
Florida Institute of Technology, Melbourne, Florida 32901
Fordham University, New York, N.Y. 10458
Gulf Coast Junior College, Panama City, Florida 32401
Hope College, Holland, Michigan 49423
Johns Hopkins University, Baltimore, Maryland 21218
Lehigh University, Bethlehem, Pennsylvania 18015
Long Island University (C.W. Post Center), Greenvale, New York
    11548
University of Maine, Orono, Maine 04473
Maritime College of the State University of New York, New York
    10017
Miami-Dade Junior College, Miami, Florida 33139
S.U.N.Y. at Stony Brook, Stony Brook, New York 11790
New York University, New York, N.Y. 10003
University of North Carolina, Chapel Hill, North Carolina 27514
Northeastern University, Boston, Massachusetts 02115
Old Dominion University, Norfolk, Virginia 23508
University of the Pacific, Stockton, California 95204
University of Rhode Island, Kingston, Rhode Island 02881
Rutgers State University of New Jersey, New Brunswick, New
    Jersey 08903

Rensselaer Polytechnic Institute, Troy, New York 12181
San Jose State College, San Jose, California 95114
Southeastern Massachusetts University, North Dartmouth,
Massachusetts 02747
St. John's University, New York, N.Y. 11432
Suffolk University, Boston, Massachusetts 02167
Texas A & M University, College Station, Texas 77840
Tufts College, Medford, Massachusetts 02155
Washington and Lee University, Lexington, Virginia 24450
Webb Institute of Naval Architecture, Glen Cove, New York 11542
University of Wisconsin, Madison, Wisconsin 53706
Woods Hole Oceanographic Institution, Woods Hole,
Massachusetts 02543

More Information on Oceanography Careers
To obtain further information, write to:

U.S. Department of Commerce
National Oceanic and Atmospheric Administration
6001 Executive Boulevard
Rockville, MD 20852

International Oceanographic Foundation
3979 Rickenbacker Causeway
Virginia Key, Miami, FL 33149

For detailed information about oceanography read:

Your Future in the Science of Oceanography by Jonathan S. Wood.
Richards Rosen Press.

Chapter VII

Conservation Scientists

For many years we took our environment for granted. There seemed to be an endless supply of trees, grass, and wildlife. The lakes, not to mention the ocean, seemed too vast ever to be polluted. Rainwater was pure. Oil and coal appeared from a bottomless pit. Nature was a limitless store of treasures to be found and raided. But recently we have begun to realize that our riches may run out. We are in danger of making our planet too exhausted to support many harmless species, and perhaps even mankind.

In this chapter you will learn about conservation scientists, who help us use our natural resources without destroying them. You will read about foresters, range managers, and soil conservationists. These scientists oversee the efficient, yet prudent use of the land that provides us with sustenance, protection, recreation, and beauty.

Conservation Sciences

Conservation is the protection and wise management of the environment. Scientists and concerned citizens practice conservation so that the environment can continue to provide for the needs of living things. Without conservation, all the resources necessary for life—air, animals, energy, minerals, plants, soil, and water—would be damaged, wasted, or destroyed.

Conservation also involves a concern for the quality of the environment so that people can enjoy living. It means keeping the environment comfortable and safe. A healthy environment contains cities that are free of junk and litter, air and water that are uncontaminated, parks that provide green space for the community, and wilderness regions where animals and plants can be safe from destruction.

It was once thought that the earth's resources were unlimited. Cities and industries thought that the rivers and oceans could consume all the wastes they could manufacture. Forestry companies thought that they could cut down all the trees, farmers thought that they could overwork the soil, hunters and trappers overkilled wildlife, and the "modernized" nations assumed that they could increasingly consume fuel. It is now apparent that people must learn to use the earth's resources much more wisely. If they do not, life may perish.

It is the responsibility of conservation scientists to help the governments, industries, and citizens of the world to understand the safeguards needed to protect the environment. Conservation scientists monitor the earth's resources, develop methods for their protection, and help manage them to assure that future needs will be met.

Conservation scientists are concerned with soil, water, air, forests, wildlife, grazing land, minerals and fuels, recreation areas, and the urban environment. Each type of conservation has its own problems and solutions, but all are related. Many occupations in the sciences involve conservation. Oceanographers are concerned with pollution of the oceans. Meteorologists are studying ways to clean the air. Biologists and medical scientists are investigating the effects of an uncontrolled industrial society on plants, animals, and man. Geologists are trying to isolate the factors that contribute to a good watershed so that fresh water can be maintained. Statisticians and mathematicians are trying to describe the parameters that can be controlled so that industrial growth can continue without destroying a resource. Chemists are developing methods for reclaiming wasted regions and for manufacturing goods that are less harmful. The list goes on and on.

Many of the scientists who work on conservation problems were trained in a traditional domain such as chemistry, life science, physics, or geology. There are some conservation occupations, however, that usually require specialized training for admission. In this chapter we shall look at three of those occupations: forester, range manager, and soil conservationist.

A. FORESTER

Our forests are a vital natural resource. They slow the runoff of rain, which provides fresh water and checks erosion. They provide homes for wildlife and offer opportunities for recreation. They provide timber for the paper, chemical, home furnishings, and construction industries. Rayon is made from material from wood, as are thousands of other useful products. Well-managed forests supply our world in many ways and provide jobs for workers in the forest-products industry.

Forests can be destroyed, too, in many ways. Trees can be cut down without new ones being planted. Forest fires can be caused by lightning or by accident. Insects and plant diseases have damaged many forests. If a forest is lost, it may take generations before it can be restored. Well-protected forests, however, can serve man indefinitely. Unlike our mineral reserves, they are a renewable resource.

Foresters are the scientists responsible for managing, developing, and protecting these lands and their resources—timber, water, wildlife, forage, and recreational areas. They may plan and supervise the cutting and planting of trees. They may study how trees grow and try to protect them from fire, harmful insects, and disease. They may supervise camps, parks, and grazing lands. They may do research, help forestry industries, or teach the public about the forests and how they can be conserved.

Forestry deals with the management of forests and forest lands so that they can provide a continuous production of goods and services. Most jobs in forestry are concerned with the management of land. An industrially owned tract may be managed by foresters for the production of timber crops for lumber, pulp and paper, or other wood products. A tract of watershed land owned by a city, state, or the Federal government, or by a water company will be managed primarily to improve and protect its values as a source of fresh water. National and State Parks are established for their scenic values and to facilitate public study and enjoyment. Foresters who work in parks help to maintain their beauty and try to ensure that they are used properly. On a wildlife refuge, a forester may want to keep the public away so that a proper habitat can be maintained.

Foresters are experts in the complex relationships between people, water, soil, animals, and plants and in the changes that can be expected in forests as one kind of tree dies and is replaced by others.

A forester plans and directs land surveys and the construction of roads, ski runs, hiking trails, swimming beaches, and campsites, as well as projects for flood control, soil conservation, and watershed improvement.

In commercial forests, foresters have a variety of responsibilities. They may have to make land surveys or supervise the cutting and planting of trees. They may need to plan and direct the reforestation of some cut-over or burned-over lands or conduct special soil erosion control or flood control measures. They also must plan and direct the control of forest fires and tree pests such as insects.

If forest land is used for grazing, the forester calculates how many wild and domestic animals it can support. The forester may seed the forest with grass or bushes suitable for forage and may reach agreements with sheep owners, for example, on seasonal use of the land.

On forest land kept as a wildlife refuge, the forester may plant berry bushes and other plants to attract birds and animals.

Some foresters specialize in one aspect of forest management, such as fire control. Some are research foresters and may work on developing faster-growing trees through plant genetics and fertilization; finding how much ground cover is needed to stop erosion from snowpack runoff; controlling insects by use of their natural enemies; or improving logging practices to waste less wood.

Foresters need an unusual combination of skills and interests. They deal with government and industrial officials, enforce forest laws, supervise and train workers, and resolve disputes between forest users. They need to be resourceful in emergencies and able to organize crews to fight fires or search parties to find lost hikers. They travel and are often required to relocate. Although city forestry (managing the mass planting of city streets, parks, and reservoirs) is a growing field, many foresters work away from metropolitan areas.

Foresters need at least a four-year college course leading to a bachelor of science degree in forestry. Practical outdoor experience is required. Most forestry schools run field camps to provide this experience. Schools may also conduct field trips giving students an opportunity to observe variations in forestry practices in different climates.

In high school, a future forester should take a full course-load in the sciences and mathematics. Communications courses, such as English and speech, are important to develop the skills needed for report writing and persuasive discussions, which are necessary to promote interest in forestry problems. Computer science is needed for biological surveys, production supervision, sales, and research.

Teaching, research, and an increasing number of other assignments require advanced degrees. After graduation, foresters may major in economics, biometrics, public relations, entomology, genetics, tree culture, botany, soil science, wildlife conservation, recreation, wood technology, or other specialties.

About 30,000 persons worked as foresters in 1980. About 10,000 worked in private industry. Most of the work in the private sector was for pulp and paper, lumber, logging, and milling companies. Nearly 6,000 foresters worked for the Federal government, primarily in the Forest Service of the Department of Agriculture. The remainder worked for state and local governments, colleges, and universities. Some were self-employed, either as consultants or forest owners.

The work of a forester in a state forest or an industrial forest is generally similar, except that in an industrial forest a greater proportion of the work would probably be devoted to the growing and harvesting of the timber. Both would involve timber inventory, harvest planning, seeding or planting, fire and pest prevention, and so on.

Forestry usually involves working in a rural or, sometimes, isolated area. A new occupation, however, called urban forestry involves working for a city or county to develop and maintain tree programs in heavily populated areas.

Research in forestry is carried on by the U.S. Forest Service, by some state agencies, by colleges and universities, and by some larger forest industry companies. The Forest Service, in the U.S. Department of Agriculture, carries out the most comprehensive research program. It maintains ten regional research units. Within each of the regions, the Forest Service maintains a number of project centers and experimental forests. The headquarters of the Forest Service are in Washington, D.C., and the world's largest institution devoted to the study of wood is at the Forest Products Laboratory in Madison, Wisconsin. This facility, run in cooperation with the University of Wisconsin, conducts research designed to increase the usefulness of forest products. The Forest Service studies a different kind of forest at its Institute of Tropical Forestry in Puerto Rico.

Some foresters work for trade associations of pulp and paper manufacturers, lumbermen, and other forestry groups. Others work for organzations that are primarily interested in conservation, such as the American Forestry Association. Many work as teachers. Some work for banks and industrial firms that need information about forests, and many work wth engineers in planning roads and construction in forest areas.

Over the next decade, there will be about 1,000 new jobs a year for foresters. Currently, more than 1,000 students each year graduate with degrees in forestry. Therefore, there is stiff competition for jobs. Opportunities will be better for those who have an advanced degree, specialized training, or several years' experience.

There may be an increase in job opportunities, however, as private owners of timberland may find an increasingly profitable market for forest products and forest services. Wood is a renewable energy resource. Some research has indicated that cottonwood forests might be able to compete with oil or coal as a fuel resource. If this trend develops, it could produce many jobs for professionals in the field. An increasing awareness by the public and private sector of environmental protection may also stimulate jobs for foresters.

B. RANGE MANAGER

Rangelands cover more than one billion acres of the United States, mostly in the Western states and Alaska. They contain many natural resources: grass and shrubs for animal grazing, habitats for livestock and wildlife, water from vast watersheds, facilities for water sports and other kinds of recreation, and valuable mineral and energy resources. Range managers manage, improve, and protect range resources.

Range managers are sometimes called range scientists, range ecologists, or range conservationists. Many range managers work for livestock ranches. They plan ways to effectively and economically use the rangelands. A range manager might determine the kind and number of animals most suited for grazing on a particular land area. After grazing, the range manager may have to reseed the area or remove brush to keep it fertile. A range conservationist is particularly aware of the balance that must be maintained between profitable grazing by herds and the needs of wildlife.

EXXON PHOTO
Range managers plan the effective use of the land.

Range managers study the rangelands and try to improve them by such techniques as controlled burning, reseeding, and control of insect pests and undesirable plants. They are often responsible, too, for providing for animal watering facilities, erosion control, and fire prevention. Range managers may also be involved in protecting and controlling timber lands, as well as outdoor recreational facilities.

Both range managers and foresters are involved in watershed management. This involves the establishment of erosion controls by planting shrubs and trees, disallowing uncontrolled timber harvests and overgrazing, and developing drainage and dam systems. The maintaining of fresh water supplies is very important to the farmer and to every citizen. Many conservation scientists work full time in protecting this resource.

About 3,500 persons worked as range managers in 1980. Most worked for the Federal government. The Forest Service and the Soil Conservation Service of the Department of Agriculture are the principal employers. The Bureau of Land Management of the Department of the Interior also hires some range managers. Range managers in state governments are usually employed in game and fish departments, state land agencies, and extension services.

An increasing number of range managers are finding work for private companies. Some are employed by livestock and agribusiness concerns. Coal and oil companies are hiring range managers to help restore the ecological balance that was disturbed by open-pit mining and other destructive drilling and mining techniques. Banks and real estate firms employ them to help develop the value of range areas.

Some range managers with advanced degrees teach and do research at colleges and universities. A few find employment with hunting clubs, conservation organizations, and other public and private agencies concerned about developing and protecting the range. Many people who study range conservation plan to manage their own livestock ranches. Most range managers work in the Western states and in Alaska.

For jobs as range managers, the usual requirement is a bachelor's degree in range management or range science. Sometimes a degree in agronomy or forestry, with coursework in range management, is acceptable. Research and college teaching positions usually require a graduate degree. In 1976 about twenty colleges and universities had degree programs in range science. A number of other schools offered some coursework in the field.

Training in range management requires a basic knowledge of biology, chemistry, physics, and mathematics. Specialized courses are taken in plant, animal, and soil sciences. Range scientists study ecology, economics, and forestry as well as wildlife management and recreation administration. Some colleges offer summer camp courses on the range, and many range managers get summer jobs with the Federal government to learn their specialty.

By 1985, the Department of Labor predicts, about 4,000 range managers will be needed. Percentagewise, this is an incredible increase. However, it only means about 100 new jobs a year. Job opportunities are expected to be good for persons with degrees in range management or range science.

Since the amount of rangeland is generally fixed, range managers will be needed to increase the output of rangelands while protecting their ecology. Cattle are spending less time on the range being fattened for slaughter; this may limit the growth of livestock herds and make finding a job as a range manager more difficult. However, legislation regarding wildlife protection and the requirements placed on mining companies to restore the ecological balance they upset should create an additional need.

C. SOIL CONSERVATIONIST

Soil conservationists provide technical assistance to farmers, ranchers, and others concerned with the proper use of one of the earth's most precious resources. Only three-tenths of the earth's surface is land; the rest is covered with water. Much of the land is too cold, too hot, too mountainous, or too wet for growing crops. As a result, less than 1 acre of land per human on the earth is arable, that is, suitable for farming. Soil conservationists are the experts who know how to develop the land so that it can produce a maximum yield for a long period of time.

Soil conservationists help farmers and other land managers develop programs that make the most productive use of land without damaging it. They do most of their work in the field. If a farmer is having trouble with erosion, the soil conservationist may suggest terracing the land or may develop a system of runoffs that will prevent too much water from soaking into the soil. Better farming methods might be suggested, or, if wind is blowing the topsoil away, hedges might be recommended as windbreaks.

The soil conservationist works with agronomists and chemists in developing fertilizers that will enrich the soil and allow continuous planting. The conservationist works with hydrologists and engineers in developing better irrigation techniques.

The conservationist works with range managers in analyzing areas where overgrazing has occurred or where fresh water is running low. Close attention is paid to weather patterns. Excessive snowfall or an early spring might cause flooding that could damage thousands of acres unless precautionary measures are taken. Similarly, droughts may require unusual methods to save a harvest. The soil conservationist must be expert in many fields, in order to work most effectively.

Most soil conservationists work for the Soil Conservation Service of the U.S. Department of Agriculture. Some work for the Department of the Interior's Bureau of Indian Affairs. Many soil conservationists for the Federal government work as advisers for Soil and Water Conservation Districts in almost every county in the country. Those employed by the Bureau of Indian Affairs generally work near or on Indian reservations, most of which are in the Western states. Soil conservationists work for state and local governments, and some teach at colleges and universities.

The Soil Conservation Service is the country's leading employer of soil conservationists. It sends out experts to help farmers and ranchers improve their lands. It also aids watershed groups, recreation agencies, construction and highway developers, and those concerned with irrigation. The Soil Conservation Service also employs agronomists, soil scientists, foresters, range conservationists, engineers, biologists, geologists, hydrologists, and agricultural economists.

Some soil conservationists are employed by rural banks, insurance firms, and mortgage companies that make loans for agricultural lands. A few work for lumber and paper companies, agribusiness industries, and other concerns that have large holdings of forested lands. Public utilities such as water companies employ soil conservationists to study and improve their watershed properties.

Very few colleges and universities offer a specific degree in soil conservation. Most soil conservationists receive bachelor's degrees in agronomy, the science of soil and crop management. A few soil conservationists have degrees in related fields of forestry, agriculture, biology, and so on. In college you should take courses in agricultural engineering, cartography (mapmaking), agricultural sciences, chemistry, biology, physics, English, and the communications arts. Of course, special training in soil chemistry is important. Advanced graduate training is required for jobs in teaching and research.

In high school prospective conservationists should take a college preparatory program. You should take all the sciences, especially chemistry and biology. It is not necessary, or perhaps even desirable, to specialize in conservation-related subjects. You will learn all you need to know in college. If you can take physics, that is preferable to an ecology or earth science class. Take as much mathematics as you can handle, and also develop your communications skills, such as writing and speaking. Conservationists must communicate well with people, since their work deals with educating farmers, ranchers, politicians, industrialists, journalists, and the public in sound conservation practices. Also, they must be able to prepare written reports and plans of programs to present to organizations and local and national government agencies.

About 8,000 soil conservationists were employed in 1980. Each year there should be new jobs for a few hundred. The Department of Agriculture is especially interested in this new field and each year is increasing the number of soil conservationists it hires.

Banks, public utilities, and other organizations that make loans on agricultural lands will continue to hire more of these specialists to evaluate their properties, make them more profitable, and help them comply with recent conservation and antipollution laws. As concern for the environment and an interest in land development grow, a larger number of colleges may add soil conservation programs to their curricula. This would increase the demand for teachers of soil conservation.

Most graduates entering the Federal government as foresters, range managers, or soil conservationists in early 1983 with only a bachelor's degree started at $13,369 a year, although those with high grades or a master's degree could start at $16,559. In 1982 the average Federal salary for foresters was about $27,900, for range conservationists about $23,700, and for soil conservationists about $26,000.

Some of the colleges and universities that offer a major in forestry are:

Auburn University, Auburn, Alabama 36830
University of California, Berkeley, California 94720
Clemson University, Clemson, South Carolina 29631
Colorado State University, Fort Collins, Colorado 80521
University of Florida, Gainesville, Florida 32611
University of Georgia, Athens, Georgia 30602
University of Idaho, Moscow, Idaho 83843
Iowa State University, Ames, Iowa 50010
University of Maine, Orono, Maine 04473
Michigan State University, East Lansing, Michigan 48824
Michigan Technological University, Houghton, Michigan 49931
Mississippi State University, State College, Mississippi 39762
University of Montana, Missoula, Montana 59801
University of New Hampshire, Durham, New Hampshire 03824
North Carolina State University, Raleigh, North Carolina 27607
Northern Arizona University, Flagstaff, Arizona 86001
Oregon State University, Corvallis, Oregon 97331
Pennsylvania State University, University Park, Pennsylvania 16802
Purdue University, Lafayette, Calumet and North Central
    Campuses, West Lafayette, Hammond, and Westville, Indiana
State University of Environmental Science and Forestry, Syracuse,
    New York 13210
University of Tennessee, Knoxville, Tennessee 37916
University of Vermont, Burlington, Vermont 05401
Virginia Polytechnical Institute, Blacksburg, Virginia 24061
Washington State University, Pullman, Washington 99163
West Virginia University, Morgantown, West Virginia 26506
University of Wisconsin, Madison, Wisconsin 53706

D. WHERE YOU CAN OBTAIN TRAINING IN THE CONSERVATION SCIENCES

Some of the colleges and universities that offer majors in the conservation sciences are:

Abilene Christian College, Abilene, Texas 79601

University of Arizona, Tucson, Arizona 85721
Bradley University, Peoria, Illinois 61606
Brevard College, Brevard, North Carolina 28712
Central Michigan University, Mount Pleasant, Michigan 48858
University of Connecticut, Storrs, Connecticut 06268
Douglas College of Rutgers University, New Brunswick, New Jersey
    08903
Duke University, Durham, North Carolina 27706
University of Florida, Gainesville, Florida 32611
University of Idaho, Moscow, Idaho 83843
Kansas State University, Manhattan, Kansas 66502
Kent State University, Kent, Ohio 44242
Louisiana Tech University, Ruston, Louisiana 71270
University of Maine, Orono, Maine 04473
Miami University, Oxford, Ohio 45056
Michigan State University, East Lansing, Michigan 48824
University of Minnesota, Minneapolis, Minnesota 55455
Murray State University, Murray, Kentucky 42071
University of Nevada, Reno, Nevada 89507
University of New Hampshire, Durham, New Hampshire 03824
New Mexico State University, Las Cruces, New Mexico 88003
North Carolina State University, Raleigh, North Carolina 27607
Ohio State University, Columbus, Ohio 43212
Purdue University, Lafayette, Calumet, North Central Campuses,
    West Lafayette, Hammond, Westville, Indiana
Rutgers University, New Brunswick, New Jersey 08903
Southern Illinois University, Edwardsville, Illinois 62025
State University of New York Agricultural and Technical College,
    Cobleskill, New York 12043
State University of New York College of Agriculture at Cornell
    University, Ithaca, New York 14850
State University of New York College of Forestry, Syracuse, New
    York 13210
Texas Tech University, Lubbock, Texas 79409
Utah State University, Logan, Utah 84322
University of Vermont, Burlington, Vermont 05401
Weber State College, Ogden, Utah 84403
West Virginia University, Morgantown, West Virginia 26506
University of Wyoming, Laramie, Wyoming 82070

E. MORE INFORMATION ON SCIENCE CAREERS

To obtain further information, write to:

Fish and Wildlife Service
U.S. Department of the Interior
Washington, DC 20240

National Wildlife Federation
1412 16th Street, NW
Washington, DC 20036

Wildlife Management Institute
709 Wire Building
Washington, DC 20005

American Forestry Association
1319 18th Street, NW
Washington, DC 20036

American Forest Institute
1619 Massachusetts Avenue, NW
Washington, DC 20036

Society of American Foresters
1010 16th Street, NW
Washington, DC 20036

U.S. Forest Service
Department of Agriculture
1621 North Kent Street
Arlington, VA 20415

American Society of Range Management
2120 South Birch Street
Denver, CO 80222

American Society of Agronomy
677 South Segoe Road
Madison, WI 53711

Soil Conservation Society of America
7515 Northeast Ankeny Road
Ankeny, IA 50021

For more detailed information you may want to read:

Career Opportunities: Ecology, Conservation and Environmental Control. J. G. Ferguson Publishing Co.

Your Future in Forestry by David Hanaburgh. Richards Rosen Press, Inc.

Chapter **VIII**

Technical Environmental Careers

A technician is a specially trained person who is assigned a highly skilled job under the supervision of a scientist, an engineer, or a supervisor with advanced training and experience. A technician understands the why and how of his or her job but is not expected to be able to interpret the results authoritatively nor to be able to develop new methods or procedures. A nurse might be described as a highly skilled and trained technician who takes care of and treats patients under the supervision of the more highly trained physician. It is the physician's responsibility to diagnose illness and prescribe the medication and procedures toward cure, but it is the nurse who carries out most of the actual treatment that heals the patient.

In this chapter, we shall look at more than thirty technical careers in water and wastewater treatment, noise control, air resources management, conservation and natural resource development, the environmental sciences and engineering, and in the energy industries. Details are given about the jobs that many of these specialists perform, how to prepare for these careers, and opportunities for employment throughout the 1980's. At the end of the chapter is a listing of some of the schools that offer training for these technical careers.

A. TECHNICAL CAREERS INVOLVING WATER AND WASTEWATER

In order to insure a safe water supply, water is purified in treatment plants to remove chemical and biological impurities and to improve its appearance, taste, color, and odor.

After the water leaves the purification plant, it is carried through a distribution of underground mains and pipes to homes, industrial plants, and agricultural lands.

Sewer systems carry used water to the wastewater treatment plant. Here it is cleaned through a series of tanks, screens, filters, and other treatment devices.

These three areas of water maintenance employ thousands of skilled people. Well-run, well-kept plants are a necessity for public health and for environmental safety. Jobs in water control activities are expected to grow at least as fast as the economy. These jobs are usually steady and not as subject to economic downturns as those in manufacturing. An increasing number of women are finding employment in water pollution control work.

For minorities and youth who do not have professional or technical training, there are some occupations that require a high school diploma or less. These entry-level jobs can provide valuable experience for young workers, and many employers help them continue their education at vocational-technical schools or junior colleges.

The greatest demand, however, will be for technicians, operators, and professionals. Jobs for the untrained and unskilled are limited in number and decreasing.

In the following sections several occupational titles that do not require a four-year college degree will be discussed. Water treatment occupations involve the processing of raw water so that it is safe for consumption by households, manufacturers, schools, and others. Wastewater treatment occupations, on the other hand, are concerned with treating water that has been used by consumers or collected from storm drainage systems and returning it to rivers and lakes.

1. Water Treatment Plant Operator

Raw water is pumped from the rivers and streams to treatment plants. Operators control equipment to remove impurities and produce clear, drinkable water. They operate and maintain pumps, agitators, and valves that move the water through the various filtering, settling, and chemical treatment processes and through the distribution system.

Operators monitor the controls that regulate the passage of the water through the filter beds and other processes. They take water samples and adjust the level of chlorine to keep the water safe. They add chemicals to disinfect, deodorize, and clarify the water. Operators use wrenches, pliers, and handtools to adjust equipment and machinery.

The duties of an operator vary, depending upon the size of the plant and the types of treatment. In treatment plants serving small communities, an operator may be responsible for keeping records, maintenance, testing of water samples, and handling complaints, as well as operating all of the equipment and machinery. In larger, metropolitan plants operators usually specialize in one area of operation.

There are more than 50,000 community water supply systems in this country and more than 200,000 water supply systems serving locations such as bottling plants, hotels, and industry.

Usually trainees for water treatment plant operator must have a high school diploma or equivalent and some experience in the operation and maintenance of mechanical equipment. Some positions are covered by civil service regulations, and applicants must pass written examinations testing their knowledge and skill before they are considered eligible for employment.

Some community or junior colleges offer two-year programs in environmental technology leading to an associate degree. These programs provide interdisciplinary, general education courses as well as technical courses in a specific field such as water pollution control. In many colleges one option is offered for operators of water and wastewater treatment plants, designed to prepare the operator for certification examinations.

The apprenticeship program for this ocupation requires 6,000 hours or approximately three years of on-the-job training and instruction.

Specialized technical training in water and wastewater treatment typically includes such courses as report writing, applied aquatic biology, water supply purification hydraulics, sanitary chemistry, codes and regulations of water and wastewater treatment, and basic courses in technical mathematics, physics, and drafting.

In most states the operator in charge must be certified. There are typically four classifications of certification based upon such factors as size of the plant, complex technologies, and experience and education of the operator.

2. Wastewater Treatment Plant Operator

Wastewater treatment plant operators are responsible for the operation of equipment that cleans water before it is released into streams or reused. It is a job on which the health and safety of the community depend. Operators control and operate the pumps, pipes, and valves that connect the collection system to the treatment plant. They monitor control panels and adjust valves and gates to regulate the flow of wastewater and waste solids through the plant. When the power flow or water flow changes, operators assess the situation, find out the causes, and take appropriate steps to remedy the problem. In some plants, they operate and maintain power generating equipment to provide heat and electricity for the plant.

Wastewater treatment plants are expensive investments involving millions of dollars. Operators inspect motors, bearings, and gear boxes for overheating and proper lubrication, check the temperatures on digester heaters, control the flow of chemicals, and perform preventive maintenance on equipment. They regularly inspect the plant and equipment for malfunction and repairs.

The job requirements and training for wastewater treatment plant operators are the same as those for water treatment plant operators. In most cases both kinds of operators work for city and state treatment plants or for state environmental health agencies. Some work for private industry and a few for the Federal government.

The Clean Water Act of 1977 should mean jobs for both kinds of operators. It is expected that there will be a continued need for trained operators throughout the 1980's.

3. Wastewater Treatment Laboratory Technician and Water Treatment Laboratory Technician

The laboratory technician in a wastewater or water treatment plant performs routine chemical, biochemical, and physical analyses of samples taken from streams, raw and treated water, sludge, and other by-products of the sewage and treatment process, in order to monitor the characteristics of the water and wastewater and to measure how effectively the treatment processes are working.

The technician collects the samples before, during, and after treatment and takes them to the laboratory for analysis. For routine tests, the technician sets up, adjusts, and operates the laboratory equipment and instrumentation such as microscopes, centrifuges, balances, scales, ovens, and other equipment in order to analyze the samples. The technician may assist the chemist in performing more difficult tests that use sophisticated equipment such as the infrared, ultraviolet, visible, and atomic absorption spectrophotometers; the gas chromatograph; and the total carbon analyzer.

Technicians perform a variety of quantitative and qualitative analyses on wastewater for such characteristics as color, turbidity, pH, alkalinity, hardness, nitrogen, oxygen demand, chlorine content, and other information. They also prepare the media and set up the equipment for the other bacteriological tests to be performed by the chemist or microbiologist.

Careful, accurate records of test results are important to make precise determinations. Technicians must be able to work well with other plant personnel; they often work under the close supervision of a chemist.

Most employers consider graduation from high school, supplemented by two years of college-level courses in chemistry or the biological sciences, a good background for working in a treatment plant. A number of community colleges offer two-year chemical technician or pollution abatement control curricula that provide suitable training. It is not unusual for someone with a baccalaureate degree in chemistry or biology to work as a technician.

The anticipated growth of new treatment plants and expansion of existing facilities should mean a continued need for laboratory technicians.

4. Treatment Plant Mechanic

Treatment plant mechanics maintain and repair the machines and equipment used to process and distribute water for human consumption and industrial use. Other treatment plant mechanics work in wastewater treatment plants where used water is cleaned before it is returned to streams and rivers.

These workers inspect the machines and equipment periodically and perform preventive maintenance work. They work with electric motors, turbines, pumps, hydraulic valves, chlorinators, limers, meters, gauges, conveyors, and blowers.

Persons in this work must be able to visualize the parts and relationships of machinery and equipment from blueprints, diagrams, and manuals. They must have above-average aptitudes in eye-hand coordination and manual and finger dexterity to work with hand and power tools such as wrenches, screwdrivers, and hoists. An interest in mechanical and craftwork is an indication of success.

Most employers prefer high school or trade school graduates. Courses in mathematics, drafting, and industrial arts are a good background for this work. Employers sometimes prefer to hire persons with one year or more of experience in some phase of mechanical repair. Some trainees learn their skills on the job under the supervision of a skilled mechanic. Others attend a vocational or technical school.

Employment in maintenance and repair work is expected to increase faster than other occupations in the economy. With experience, a mechanic could become a supervisor. Additional experience and education may lead to certification in plant operations and a high-level job as a superintendent of a treatment plant.

Water Pollution Control Technician

A growing number of technicians are engaged in various activities related to water pollution control projects. They conduct field tests, surveys, and investigations to obtain data for use by environmental, engineering, and scientific personnel in determining sources and methods of controlling pollutants in water.

These technicians collect water samples from streams, rivers, lakes, or raw, semiprocessed, or processed water, industrial wastewater, and other sources. Sometimes technicians conduct physical and chemical field tests to identify the composition of the sample. They must take precise, accurate measurements. Certain data such as temperature, turbidity, and pressure must be measured and recorded in the natural environment to obtain accurate data. They must maintain clear and accurate records of their work.

Persons can qualify for these jobs with an associate in arts degree with specialization in chemical technology, science, or a related field, which can be obtained at a community college. Technicians are usually provided on-the-job training under a professional engineer or scientist. For advancement, most employers require a bachelor's degree in science or engineering.

There has been an increased demand for technicians in private industry and consulting firms to assist professionals in the data collection and verification for a variety of water pollution control projects.

6. Estuarine Resource Technician

America's coastlines are fringed by sprawling areas where salt and fresh water meet. These areas, or estuaries, commonly identified as bays, inlets, sounds, sloughs, salt marshes, and lagoons, are fertile, productive zones where a variety of fish, shellfish, migratory birds, and animals live.

Estuarine resource technicians work with scientists and oceanographers to study a variety of complex environmental problems. They work in biological and chemical laboratories to investigate problems of water pollution as it affects different forms of life in estuaries. They perform a variety of field and laboratory work using sampling and anlytical methods employed by water-quality laboratories.

A person with an associate in arts degree with emphasis on mathematics and the sciences can usually qualify for this technician work.

There is a need in this area for a limited number of research assistants and technicians. These positions are found in private industry and with Federal and state government agencies.

7. Water and Sewer Drafter

These drafters perform highly specialized drafting work. In the construction of wastewater treatment plants, water purification plants, and other water pollution control projects, there is an intricate network of complex piping systems for the control of water, wastewater, sludge, and gas.

Drafters prepare plans and detailed drawings of the piping systems of water and sewer projects. These drawings are based on the rough sketches, plans, and specifications prepared by engineers, architects, and designers. The drafter must be knowledgeable about a wide variety of piping components and other fittings and show this information on the plans and specifications. The final drawings contain a detailed view of the plans, indicating dimensions and tolerances, joining requirements, and other information.

Graduation from a technical or vocational school with an associate in arts degree or a certificate in drafting is usually the minimum educational requirement. A typical program includes courses in English and technical report writing; basics in graphics, including the use of drafting instruments, lettering, and engineering drawing; descriptive geometry; perspective drawing; technical mathematics; and physics.

A drafter could begin as a tracer, making minor corrections and tracing drawings under the supervision of a senior drafter.

In many areas, experienced piping drafters are in demand. Jobs are expected to increase with new construction and expansion of water treatment plants.

8. Other Occupations

Industrial waste inspectors inspect industrial and commercial waste treatment and disposal facilities and investigate sources of pollutants in municipal sewage and storm drainage systems. They are needed to enforce industrial waste discharge ordinances and laws.

Industrial waste samplers take samples from streams and raw and treated wastewater for analysis by laboratory technicians and chemists in a wastewater treatment plant. They dip buckets or other vessels into pipelines, tanks, streams, sewers, drainage basins, and so on. They note the presence of oil, discoloration of water, sludge, and rate of flow. They do routine tests of acidity, alkalinity, temperature, turbidity, and other information. The demand for samplers is limited, however.

Photo-inspection technicians operate a 35-mm camera or a television camera to conduct internal inspections of sewer lines in order to determine the condition of the pipes and the need for repairs. The camera is usually attached to a cable that moves remotely inside the pipes taking pictures at designated intervals. This job is typically found in communities with large sewage systems serving populations over 100,000.

Ditch riders, or canal tenders, control irrigation systems that convey water to farms for irrigating fields and crops. Ditch riders contact water users to determine the quantity of water needed and the time and duration of delivery. After the irrigation season has passed, ditch riders spend most of their time cleaning ditches, raising ditch banks, repairing structures, and other maintenance work. These jobs are located in agricultural areas. Usually, no previous training is required, and a new worker can learn this job with six months of on-the-job training. There will probably

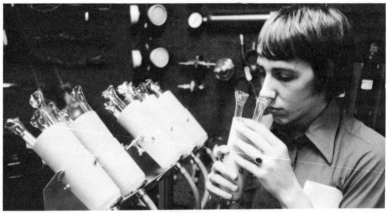

A technician judges the odor emanating from wastewater samples.

be a limited number of openings for this career as workers retire or transfer.

Watershed tenders control the equipment that regulates the flow in reservoirs. Reservoirs are artificial lakes where water is collected and kept until needed. The tender releases the water during periods of demand, and then, when the demand diminishes, closes the valves so that the reservoir can refill with water. Most employers prefer persons with a high school education for this important job. Machine shop skills are especially valuable. Only a few openings will develop for this occupation.

B. TECHNICAL CAREERS IN NOISE CONTROL

Noise control is a relatively new and growing field, as more people become aware of the need for healthful surroundings. We know that noise has damaging effects: people become irritable, students have trouble studying, conversation is difficult, and the recuperative value of sleep is interfered with even when sleep is possible. Noise can raise blood pressure, heartbeat, and cholesterol levels. In addition, noise can permanently damage hearing. About 16 million Americans work on jobs where the noise level is so high that their hearing is in danger.

Since noise control is a relatively new field, most of the workers now in it were trained in other fields and have other responsibilities, such as air resources, highway planning, or occupational health. In the future, more workers may specialize in noise control.

It is likely that more noise technicians and hearing-test technicians will be employed when the hearing provisions of the Occupational Safety and Health Act are fully enforced. The greatest number of openings may be in schools and private practice.

1. Audiometrist (Hearing-test Technician or Hearing Conservationist)

A first step in hearing conservation programs is the giving of routine hearing tests to large numbers of workers, schoolchildren, or others.

Audiometrists assist audiologists and physicians by giving screening tests to find persons with hearing loss who need further attention. Audiometrists handle delicate testing equipment and must record results legibly and accurately.

No specific educational background is required of these technicians. They are either trained on the job by an audiologist or given an intensive three-day course covering their responsibilities and techniques. They learn how we hear, the principles of noise measurement and control, and the laws regarding hearing-loss compensation.

Audiometrists work in schools, industries, the military services, and public hearing-conservation programs.

2. Noise Technician

Noise technicians operate sound-testing instruments to measure and analyze noise. The data they collect is used for research, for writing environmental impact statements, and for enforcing noise regulations.

Technicians may set up their instruments near an airfield, in an office building, on a highway, or in a factory. Some test manufactured products, such as trucks, snowmobiles, lawnmowers, chain saws, and industrial vacuum cleaners. Others respond to complaints about noise and determine whether or not a law is being violated.

Noise technicians work for either industry or government. In government, some issue summonses and are called noise control officers or inspectors.

The minimum educational requirement for these technicians is a high school diploma with good skills in arithmetic. The training is usually given on the job or in an intensive three- to five-day course. The main part of the training covers methods of measuring noise and the care and operation of delicate electronic instruments.

Openings for noise technicians will depend upon enforcement activities of such agencies as the Occupational Safety and Health Administration and the Environmental Protection Agency.

C. TECHNICAL CAREERS IN AIR RESOURCE MANAGEMENT

Each year in the United States, smokestacks and tailpipes release into the air we breathe 200 million tons of fumes and soot. This pollution reduces the distance we can see, corrodes buildings, strips the leaves from plants, burns our eyes, and increases our chances of suffering from lung and heart disease or cancer.

Technicians are needed to assist the professionals who are trying to find ways to reduce the polluting effects of cars, trucks, factories, and power plants. Technicians are used to collect data on air pollution and to perform routine tests.

1. Air Technician

Air technicians collect samples of outdoor air or of pollutants, such as fumes or dust entering the air. They do routine tests on the samples, using special measuring instruments; record the amount of pollutants; and supply this information to an engineer. Technicians are responsible for the frequent calibration or checking of their instruments to insure accuracy.

3M PHOTO

A field testing technician operates an air sampling instrument while collecting total particulate emissions from a boiler stack during an engineering pilot study.

Some air technicians keep watch on pollution sources, such as inspecting smoke-control equipment in factories or testing engine exhaust from motor vehicles. Some operate vans equipped with built-in electronic instruments and investigate air-pollution complaints or use the vans to gather information on air-pollution in traffic.

Air technicians are usually required to have two years of college-level technical education or technical experience. This education may be in technical school, community college, or college, with such courses as engineering, physical science, and mathematics. Practical experience may be in either analytical laboratory or mechanical and electrical work. Particularly desirable is experience with instrumentation or with motor vehicle maintenance.

Air technicians are employed by city, county, state, and Federal governments. They work for the departments of health, environment, transportation, or traffic. Some are employed by private engineering consultants who specialize in environmental problems. A limited number of technician jobs will be available. For promotion, a four-year college degree with a major in engineering or physical science is usually necessary.

2. Meteorological Technician

A few air technicians are assigned to assist the meteorologists who forecast air-pollution levels. These technicians observe sky and visibility conditions, read weather instruments, receive weather information from teletype and facsimile machines, and enter information on graphs and maps.

Technicians measure and record temperature, pressure, humidity, wind speed and direction, and precipitation. To get information on the upper layers of air, they float balloons equipped with miniature radio transmitters, record the transmitted data, and calculate the height of balloons using the triangulation method with trigonometric tables or calculators.

The technician is required to have either two years of technical training or an associate degree in engineering, mathematics, or physics. Very few openings are expected in this field.

D. TECHNICAL CAREERS IN CONSERVATION AND NATURAL RESOURCE DEVELOPMENT

Workers in conservation and natural resource development help us use our land and wildlife without destroying them. If trees are cut, other trees are planted. Streams are restocked with fish. If a meadow is used for grazing, the number of animals on the land is controlled so that plants are not trampled until nothing will grow.

Animals and plants, like people, need an environment in which to live, a habitat supplying food and shelter. When a forest or stream is destroyed, the animals and flora that naturally live in it are destroyed too, and we lose another jewel in our limited treasure trove.

It is impossible to say that any form of life is useless. Plants and animals depend upon each other in a complex web of relationships. When one plant or animal becomes extinct, others are affected.

Foresters, wildlife biologists, fish biologists, park rangers, conservation officers, and land planners have the complicated responsibility of saving natural resources while still making it possible to use and enjoy them.

Occupations in land, fish, and animal management, once thought of as jobs for men, are now open to women as well. Many women, for example, are enrolled in forestry courses, and it is no longer unusual to see women working as park rangers.

Job openings for most of these occupations, however, are limited and competitive. At the technical level some of the openings are temporary or seasonal and, because there is a shortage of openings for such jobs as forester, technicians must compete with overqualified professionals for technical-level openings. Even for professionals, such as biologists, openings are few.

1. Conservation Officer

Conservation officers patrol fish and wildlife areas to protect natural resources so that people have an opportunity to enjoy them. They travel over a large area on foot, by patrol car, horseback, motorboat, or sometimes by airplane or helicopter. Emphasis is on voluntary compliance, and much effort is on educational activities, explaining laws to visitors and giving talks to groups.

Conservation officers check fishing and hunting licenses; investigate illegal burning and boating and hunting accidents; and give first aid to accident victims. They may assist wildlife biologists by collecting information on the presence of food and cover for game. They may plant food patches for wildlife or assist in a fish census or animal rescue operation. They may patrol shellfish areas and board commercial fishing and lobster boats to inspect for violations.

High school graduation is required for this occupation, plus either experience or education in law enforcement, farming, or resource management. The education requirement can usually be met through special programs at technical or community colleges.

Most conservation officers work for state conservation departments, which usually hire state residents familiar with local conditions and animals. A small number work for the U.S. Fish and Wildlife Service. Openings are limited, and future Federal hiring is expected to be low.

2. Fish Culturist

The fish culturist supervises the day-to-day operations of a fish hatchery, following procedures determined by a fish biologist. The technician oversees the temperature, flow, and other conditions of the indoor tanks and outdoor ponds. If a system fails, hundreds of thousands of fish may die. Usually the fish culturist must live next to the hatchery and be on call 24 hours a day.

Care of the fish varies with the time of year and runs through a cycle. In the spawning season, eggs and sperm are pressed from mature fish and mixed to fertilize the eggs. Eggs are incubated in trays placed in running water. Growing fish are nourished by the culturist, and are moved to larger tanks as they grow. The last step is transporting the fish to lakes, streams, and reservoirs.

At least one year of practical experience in fishery work is required for a permanent job. Some fish culturists are high school graduates who have on-the-job training, but many have two-year associate degrees in fisheries management or biology. A bachelor's degree is now a requirement for some openings. Experience with high-voltage equipment, plumbing, machinery repairs, or the use of farm equipment is helpful.

Fish culturists work in state and Federal hatcheries. A few may work for private concerns, research organizations, and aquariums. Very few openings are expected in this career.

3. Forestry Technician

Forestry technicians, sometimes called forestry aides, assist foresters in the care and management of forest lands and their resources. These nonprofessional workers may cruise timber, look out for fires, scale logs, assist in surveys, or guard forest areas. Technicians work on many forest improvement projects. They inspect trees for disease and other problems and record their findings. They work to prevent flood damage and soil erosion and seek ways to increase the quality of water in the forest. Technicians may maintain forest areas for hunting, camping, hiking, and other recreational activities. They may aid in the planting of new trees after a fire or a major harvest.

Although college is generally not a required condition for a job as a forestry techncian, the keen job competition favors those with some junior college training. In 1976 about eighty technical institutes, junior or community colleges, and universities offered forestry technician training; fifty-three of these institutions were recognized by the Society of American Foresters. At these schools, students receive general academic coursework, including biology, mathematics, and botany, and forest technology courses such as land surveying, tree identification, aerial photograph interpretation, and timber harvesting. In addition, forestry technicians usually spend a summer at a forest or camp learning specialized techniques firsthand.

About 12,000 persons worked full time as forestry technicians in 1980.

Over the next decade about 500 new jobs a year should develop. In addition, there were about 11,000 temporary jobs, primarily with the Federal and state governments, during the summer and in the spring and fall seasons. Nearly half the year-round total worked in private industry. There may be a rapid increase in the employment of forestry technicians, since they can perform many of the routine tasks now carried out by more highly paid professional foresters. This will allow the forester more time to devote to supervisory work and to the general management of the forest.

4. Park Ranger

Park rangers patrol and maintain parks and explain park facilities to visitors. Their job is to protect public parks and the people who use them. They patrol the parks by vehicle or on foot. They watch for illegal hunting, cutting of trees, vandalism, and excessive noise. The park ranger observes trees and wildlife and reports any evidence of insect infestation or disease. Hazards such as avalanche conditions, flooding, washed-out roads, weakened guardrails, or undercut trails are reported immediately to the supervisor.

Duties include participation in the educational program, giving prepared speeches on natural and historic features of the area, guiding visitors on nature trails, and answering the public's questions. The ranger teaches safety and responds to emergencies and accidents.

Minimum requirements are a high school diploma, a driver's license, and one year of experience in a related field. College education in natural science, history, archaeology, police science, or park and recreation management may be substituted for experience.

Opportunities for park rangers are limited and competitive. It is anticipated that there may be an increasing number of openings because of growing interest in outdoor recreation and conservation. Information on Federal openings can be obtained by writing to the National Park Service, U.S. Department of the Interior, 18th and C Streets, NW, Washington, DC 20240.

E. TECHNICAL CAREERS IN THE ENVIRONMENTAL SCIENCES AND ENGINEERING

Technicians help scientists and engineers carry out their research and studies involving the environment. They may collect samples, carry out routine analyses, set up monitoring equipment, take measurements, record data, plot graphs, prepare samples for microscopic study, or be assigned field investigations. The scientist or engineer is specially trained to understand the reasons for certain tests and experiments and is capable of evaluating the research; however, the technician often can be trusted to carry out the most detailed and accurate tests prescribed. The technician becomes a member of a team of investigators trying to protect the planet.

1. Chemical Laboratory Technician

Chemical laboratory technicians assist chemists by maintaining equipment, weighing and mixing chemicals, and performing routine chemical and physical tests. Chemical laboratory technicians work in many pollution control areas. They may test filter papers exposed to air pollutants from car exhausts or smokestack emissions. The laboratory technicians calculate how much of a pollutant is present in the air. They may analyze samples from the soil, water, seawater, industrial waste, or sewage.

Chemical laboratory technicians set up, adjust, and operate laboratory equipment and instrumentation such as the microscope, centrifuge, agitator, scales, ovens, spectrophotometer, gas chromatograph, and mass spectrometer. They compare their results to standardized samples of known composition and record their data for the scientist or engineer.

Many community colleges offer two-year programs for chemical technicians. The student studies inorganic chemistry, organic chemistry, and quantitative and qualitative analysis. In addition, the student must be good in math and have good mechanical skills. Many graduates of associate in arts degree programs continue, part time, toward a baccalaureate degree while employed.

There is usually a demand for qualified chemical laboratory technicians in private industry, environmental engineering and research firms, health agencies, and treatment plants, and there should be some limited openings with government agencies.

2. Engineering Technician

Engineering technicians assist professional engineers. They apply their skills to various projects, such as the preparation and review of plans and specifications for the construction of water distribution systems, swimming pools, purification plants, and wastewater treatment facilities. They may work on projects dealing with large ecosystems, or they may specialize in noise, air, or water pollution control.

Engineering technicians may review construction details or inspect sites where new operations are being carried out. They may be involved in predicting the quantities of materials required for a project or the cost of repairs and maintenance. Some engineering technicians conduct stream surveys and collect water samples. Others inspect public water supplies or investigate complaints of pollution or environmental crisis, such as a fish kill.

Technician positions require varying combinations of education and experience. Usually some college-level coursework in drafting or engineering technology is required. Curricula in technical and community colleges prepare a student, but some employers might insist on work experience or a bachelor's degree. Most technicians continue working toward an engineering degree while on the job.

Engineering technicians are employed by Federal, state, and local pollution control agencies. Others work for consulting engineering firms, architectural firms, municipal treatment plants, and private industry. There should be jobs for engineering technicians, though some may be temporary to meet production deadlines.

3. Radiation Laboratory Technician

The radiation laboratory technician is usually employed in a radiological health laboratory and is concerned with the analysis of samples of material for radioactivity levels. These technicians may analyze samples of water, silt, earth, vegetation, or construction materials used in a reactor. Sometimes these technicians are called radiation monitors.

Monitors calculate the amount of time that personnel may safely work in contaminated areas. They may collect and test radiation detectors worn by workers as film badges and pocket detection chambers. They may also give instructions in radiation safety procedures and prescribe special clothing requirements and other safety precautions for workers entering radiation zones.

The minimum education requirement is usually the completion of an associate degree in radiation technology. Job opportunities are best in the public sector, where technician-level jobs may be structured so as to have promotional ladders to professional level as the employee receives advanced education, training, and experience.

4. Entomology Field Assistant

Field assistants work under the direction of entomologists in trapping insects and in fumigating and spraying. They assign work and give instructions to laborers on pest control projects and personally work with the crews.

With increased experience, field assistants take on more responsible work with less direction from the entomologist. Assistants survey and record information on insect infestations, take samples of insect populations, estimate and order chemicals and equipment in control projects, and help in the evaluation of the control measures taken.

Most employers require at least two years' experience in agricultural work, part of which must have been directly associated with insect control duties. Many employers prefer that these technicians have some community college coursework in biology. Opportunities are found with local and state government agencies.

5. Vector Control Assistant (Epidemiological Assistant)

Vector control assistants assist professional staff responsible for preventing and controlling vectors (disease-transmitting organisms) and hosts of diseases important to public health. The work can be varied and can include participation in investigations, identification, control, and prevention duties.

Vector control assistants learn the principles and techniques of biological investigation, such as collection of specimens, use and care of laboratory equipment, laboratory techniques, identification of species, and preparation of reports. They assist in surveys of rodents, flies, aquatic insects, and in special problems of solid waste disposal.

Vector control assistants usually work for public health agencies and may be hired with either an associate degree in the biological sciences or some college work in biology with one to two years' experience in a related work area. Opportunities should continue to be good for this work.

F. TECHNICAL CAREERS IN THE ENERGY INDUSTRIES

As the nation continues to meet the growing need for energy at a time when traditional energy resources are dwindling, more and more people are finding jobs in energy-related industries. This trend is expected to continue throughout the 80's.

1. Mining and Petroleum Industry

The mining and petroleum industry employed about 900,000 workers in 1980. Coal mining accounted for over one-fourth of the industry's workers. The remaining workers were in metal mining and quarrying and nonmetallic mineral mining.

Blue-collar workers, craft workers and operatives, account for nearly 70 percent of the industry's employment. Operatives, the largest occupational group, include oil well drillers, mining machinery operators, and truck and tractor drivers. Craft workers, the second-largest group, include both mechanics and repairers who maintain mining and oil drilling equipment and operators of power shovels and bulldozers in open-pit mining. Large numbers of pumpers, gaugers, and engine workers hold jobs in the production and transportation of petroleum and natural gas.

The industry's white-collar employees are divided among three occupational groups—professional and technical, clerical, and managerial workers.

Professional and technical workers are concentrated largely in petroleum and gas extraction. Most engineers, geologists, and technicians are engaged in exploration and research. The clerical employees are mostly secretaries, office machine operators, and typists.

Employment in coal mining and in petroleum and natural gas extraction should increase rapidly as the nation strives to become self-sufficient in energy sources. Employment in metal mining is also expected to grow. Employment in quarrying and nonmetallic mining, on the other hand, is expected to decline as labor-saving equipment leads to higher output with fewer workers.

The petroleum refining industry forms the link between crude oil production and the distribution and consumption of petroleum products. Products refined from crude oil supply the fuels and lubricants used for all modes of transportation, for heat in homes, factories, and other structures, and for fuel to generate electric power. In addition, basic petroleum compounds are used to manufacture hundreds of everyday products such as synthetic rubber, fertilizers, plastics, and fibers.

About half of the workers in a refinery are involved in the operation of the plant. In modern plants, refinery operators monitor instruments on panels that show the entire operation of all processing units in the refinery. They also patrol units to check their operating condition. Refinery operator helpers make adjustments for changes in temperature, pressure, and oil flow.

Other plant workers may include stillpump operators and pumpers who maintain and operate pumps that control all production throughout the refinery. Treaters are employees who operate equipment to remove impurities from gasoline, oil, and other products. In automated plants, computers may do the work of pumpers and treaters. Operators, then, monitor the computers to spot potential problem areas and make routine checks of the refinery to make sure that valves are operating properly.

Almost 14 percent of the workers in petroleum refineries are scientists, engineers, and technicians. Among them are chemists, chemical engineers, mechanical engineers, environmental engineers, laboratory technicians, and drafters. Chemists and laboratory technicians control the quality of petroleum products by making tests and analyses to determine chemical and physical properties. Some chemists and chemical

8

engineers develop and improve products and processes. Laboratory technicians assist chemists in research projects or do routine testing and sample taking. Some engineers design chemical processing equipment and plant layout, and others supervise refining processes. Environmental engineers and technicians supervise and improve treatment and disposal of refinery wastewater and gases. Drafters prepare plans and drawings needed in refinery construction and maintenance.

Refining companies employ other kinds of white-collar workers. Among the professional workers needed to keep a refinery going are managers, accountants, purchasing agents, lawyers, computer programmers, systems analysts, and personnel and training specialists. Typists, secretaries, bookkeepers, keypunch operators, and business machine operators provide clerical support.

2. Electric Utilities

The delivery of electricity to users at the instant they need it is the task of the electric utility industry. Since electricity cannot be stored efficiently but must be used as it is produced, an electric utility system must have sufficient capacity to meet peak consumer needs at any time.

Producing and distributing large quantities of electrical energy involve many processes and activities. The first step in providing electrical energy occurs in a generating station or plant, where huge generators convert mechanical energy into electricity. Electricity is produced primarily in steam-powered generating plants that use coal, gas, oil, or nuclear energy for fuel. In addition, a considerable amount of electricity is produced in hydroelectric generating stations that use water power to operate the turbines.

After electricity is generated, it passes through transformers where the voltage is increased so that the electricity may travel long distances without excessive loss of power. Next the electricity passes onto transmission lines that carry it from the generating plant to substations, where the voltage is decreased and passed on to the distribution networks serving individual customers.

In 1980, almost 600,000 people worked in the electric power industry. Many different types of workers are required in the industry. About 40 percent of the employees work in occupations related to the generation, transmission, and distribution of electricity, and in customer service occupations. The industry also employs large numbers of workers in engineering, scientific, administrative, sales, clerical, and maintenance occupations.

Engineers plan generating plant construction and additions, interconnections of complex systems, and installation of new transmission and distribution systems and equipment. They supervise construction, develop improved operating methods, and test the efficiency of the many types of electrical equipment. Engineers help select plant sites, types of fuel, and types of plants. They also help industrial and commercial customers make the best use of electric power.

Because of the enormous amount of record-keeping required, electric utilities employ many administrative and clerical personnel. Large numbers of stenographers, typists, bookkeepers, office machine operators, file clerks, account and auditing clerks, and cashiers are employed. An increasing amount of this work is being performed by computers, so that keypunch operators, computer programmers, and systems analysts are being hired by electric utilities. Administrative employees include accountants, personnel officers, purchasing agents, and lawyers.

A considerable number of workers test, maintain, and repair equipment. Among the more important skilled workers are electricians, instrument repairers, industrial machinery repairers, machinists, pipe fitters, welders, and boilermakers.

3. Nuclear Energy

In 1980 about 350,000 people worked in nuclear energy activities. Most were employed in the design and engineering of nuclear facilities and in the development and manufacture of nuclear weapons and nuclear reactors and their components. Many persons also were involved in research and development of nuclear energy. Most nuclear energy workers are scientists, engineers, technicians, and craft workers, mainly because much of the work is still in the research and development phase.

Although many engineers working in the nuclear energy field are trained in nuclear technology, engineers trained in other branches are also employed. Mechanical engineers are the largest single group, but many electrical, electronic, chemical, civil, and metallurgical engineers work alongside the nuclear engineering staff. Many do research and development work; others design nuclear reactors, nuclear instruments, and other equipment.

Research laboratories and other organizations that do nuclear energy work employ scientists in basic and applied nuclear research. Most are physicists and chemists, but mathematicians, biologists, and metallurgists also do nuclear energy research.

Large numbers of engineering and science technicians, drafters, and radiation monitors assist the engineers and scientists in conducting research and in designing and testing equipment.

Many craft workers build equipment for experimental and pilot work and maintain the complex equipment and machinery. Many maintenance mechanics and all-around machinists work in most nuclear energy activities.

4. Opportunities in Technical Energy Careers

As nuclear development increases, the need for technicians will increase, especially for those technicians performing highly skilled tests. Reactor operators and instrumentation control technicians are two careers for which there will be a great demand if nuclear power plants now under construction and planned are licensed.

If synthetic fuel production becomes a large-scale industry in the United States, chemical and engineering technicians will be in special demand. Mining engineers, mechanics, and equipment operators will be required in the coal industry.

The Department of Energy released in 1980 estimates of where there will be a need for jobs in technical energy careers. In this table if there is a demand for people a • is placed in the box. If there is a significant demand, then you will find ••.

Technical Energy Careers

Technicians:	Coal	Nuclear	Oil and Gas Exploration and Extraction	Oil Shale	Synthetic Fuel from Coal	Fossil-Fueled Electric Power Plants	Petroleum Refineries
Chemical			••	•		•	••
Draftsman			•			•	•
Electrical			•			••	•
Engineering			•	•	•	•	
Health	•		•	•	•		•
Industrial							•
Instrumentation Control		••					
Radiation Monitor		•					
Reactor Operator		••					
Surveyor	•	•	••	•			
Welder	•		•	•			••

For blue-collar and craft jobs in the energy industries, the job outlook is as follows:

Job Categories	Coal	Nuclear	Oil and Gas Exploration and Extraction	Oil Shale	Synthetic Fuel from Coal	Fossil-Fueled Electric Power Plants	Petroleum Refineries
Asbestos Worker		••			•		•
Boilermaker		••	•			•	
Carpenter	•	••		•	•	•	
Cement-Concrete Finisher		•					
Draftsman	•	••	••	•		••	••
Driller (Crew Chief Operator)	•	•	••	•			
Electrician	•	••	•	••	•	••	
Laborer	•	••	•	•	•	••	•
Ironworker		•				•	
Machinist	•		•		•		••
Mechanic	••	••	••	••	••	••	••
Millwright		•			•	•	••
Mine Operative	••	••	••	•			
Rig Foreman (Tool Pusher)			••				
Service Worker (Roustabout)			••	••			
Sheetmetal Worker			•		•		•
Steam and Pipe Fitters	•	••	••	••	••	••	••
Surveyor	•		•	•	•		•

In 1982 average starting salaries for technicians with associate degrees were as follows:

Agricultural Technician	$11,000
Animal Science Technician	12,500
Biology Technician	13,800
Chemistry Technician	15,000
Engineering Technician	13,800

Drafter $12,000
Conservation Technician   11,000

The salaries for experienced technicians working for the Federal
government were as follows:
Physical Science Technician $18,000
Meteorological Technician   21,000
Forestry Technician   16,000
Biological Technician   16,000
Engineering Technician   19,000

Many technicians receive an hourly wage that ranges from $8 to $18
per hour depending on experience and the difficulty of the work.

G. SOME EDUCATIONAL INSTITUTIONS THAT OFFER TWO-YEAR AND CERTIFICATE PROGRAMS IN ENVIRONMENTAL FIELDS

Aiken Technical Education Center
Engineering and Industrial
  Technologies Division
P.O. Drawer 696
Aiken, South Carolina 29801

Anne Arundel Community College
Department of Environmental
  Research Protection and
  Development
Arnold, Maryland 21012

Anson Technical Institute
Agriculture Department
P.O. Box 68
Ansonville, North Carolina 28007

Bergen Community College
Department of Biological Sciences
Environmental Technology
  Program
400 Paramus Road
Paramus, New Jersey 07652

Berkshire Community College
Environmental Science Department
West Street
Pittsfield, Massachusetts 01201

Bluefield State College
Engineering Technology
  Department
  (Mining Option)
Bluefield, West Virginia 24701

Boston University
Center for Energy Studies
Engineering Department
110 Cunnington Street
Boston, Massachusetts 02215

Bristol Community College
Engineering Department
Fall River, Massachusetts 02720

Butte Community College
Mathematics, Technology and
  Telecommunications Department
Pentz and Clark Roads
Route 1, Box 183A
Oronville, California 95965

Carl Sandburg College
Vocational/Technical Education
  Department
Box 104
South Lake Storey Road
Galesburg, Illinois 61401

Casper College
Division of Technology Trades and
Industry (Coal Field Technology;
Petroleum Engineering
Technology)
125 College Drive
Casper, Wyoming 83601

Central Florida Community College
Radiological Health Technology
Department
P.O. Box 1388
Ocala, Florida 32670

Central New England College
Engineering Department
768 Main Street
Worcester, Massachusetts 01608

Central Technical Community
College
Environmental Technology
Department
Box 1024
Hastings, Nebraska 68901

Central New England College
Engineering Department
768 Main Street
Worcester, Massachusetts 01608

Central Technical Community
College
Environmental Technology
Department
Box 1024
Hastings, Nebraska 68901

Central Virginia Community
College
Engineering and Technology
Division
Wards Road South
P.O. Box 4098
Lynchburg, Virginia 24502

Charles County Community College
Pollution Abatement Technology
Department
La Plata, Maryland 20646

Chattanooga State Technical
Community College
Division of Engineering
Technologies
4501 Amnicola Highway
Chattanooga, Tennessee 37406

Chemeketa Community College
Trade and Industry Department
P.O. Box 1007
Salem, Oregon 97308

Citrus College
Public Services Department
18824 East Foothill Blvd.
Azusa, California 91702

City University of New York
College of Staten Island
Environmental Health Science
Program
Saint George Campus
130 Stuyvesant Place
Staten Island, New York 10301

Clackamas Community College
Water Quality Curriculum
Department
19600 South Molalla Avenue
Oregon City, Oregon 97045

Claremore Junior College
Occupational-Technical Programs in
Environmental Science
Claremore, Oklahoma 74017

Clatsop Community College
Program on Pest Management for
Plant Protection
Astoria, Oregon 97103

College of the Canyons
Environmental Control Department
26455 North Rockwell Canyon
   Road
Valencia, California 91355

College of Eastern Utah
Division of Applied Sciences
   (Mining Technology)
451 East Fourth North
Price, Utah 84501

Colorado Mountain College
Environmental Protection
   Technology
Leadville, Colorado 80461

Community College of Allegheny
   County
Department of Engineering
Environment Technology
Boyce Campus
595 Beatly Road
Monroeville, Pennsylvania 15146

Community College of Baltimore
Division of Engineering, Marine
   and Maritime Technologies
2901 Liberty Heights Avenue
Baltimore, Maryland 21215

Community College of Beaver
   County
Nuclear Quality Assurance
   Technology Program
College Drive
Monaca, Pennsylvania 15061

Community College of Denver
Division of Service Occupations
12600 West 6th Avenue
Denver, Colorado 80201

Connors State College
Social Sciences Division
Water Way Law Enforcement
Warner, Oklahoma 74469

Consumnes River College
Agriculture Department
8401 Center Parkway
Sacramento, California 95823

Contra Costa College
Technical and Industrial Division
2600 Mission Bell Drive
San Pablo, California 94806

County College of Morris
Chemistry/Chemical Technology
   Department
Route 10 and Center Grove Road
Randolph Township, New Jersey
   07801

Delaware Technical and
   Community College
Applied Sciences Department
P.O. Box 897
Denney's Road and U.S. Route 13
Dover, Delaware 19901

Delaware Technical and
   Community College
Civil Engineering Technology
   Department
Southern Campus
Box 610
Georgetown, Delaware 19947

Dundalk Community College
Math/Science Division
7200 Sollers Point Road
Baltimore, Maryland 21222

Elgin Community College
Technical/Vocational Program
1700 Spartan Drive
Elgin, Illinois 60120

Fayetteville Technical Institute
Department of Environmental
   Engineering Technology
P.O. Box 5236
Fayetteville, North Carolina 28303

Ferris State College
School of Allied Health (Pesticide
Technology)
Big Rapids, Michigan 49307

Florence-Darlington Technical
College
Division of Engineering Technology
(Nuclear Specialization)
P.O. Drawer 8000
Florence, South Carolina

Fresno City College
Water Utility Science Department
1101 East University Avenue
Fresno, California 93741

Fullerton College
Life Science Department
321 E. Chapman Avenue
Fullerton, California 92634

Gadsden State Junior College
Division of Vocational/Technical
Education
George Wallace Drive
Gadsden, Alabama 35903

Garrett Community College
Division of Mathematics
Science and Environmental Studies
McHenry, Maryland 21541

Georgia Institute of Technology
College of Engineering
225 North Avenue, N.W.
Atlanta, Georgia 30332

Harrisburg Area Community
College
Division of Mathematics, Physical
Sciences and Engineering
3300 Cameron St. Road
Harrisburg, Pennsylvania 17110

Hartford State Technical College
Nuclear Technology Department
401 Flatbush Avenue
Hartford, Connecticut 06106

Hazard Community College
Coal Mining Technology Program
Hazard, Kentucky 41701

Hinds Junior College
Chemistry Department
Raymond Campus
Raymond, Mississippi 39154

Hofstra University
Continuing Engineering Education
Department
Hempstead, New York 11550

Holyoke Community College
Division of Health Related
Programs
303 Homestead Avenue
Holyoke, Massachusetts 01040

Imperial Valley College
Water Treatment Technology
Department
P.O. Box 158
Imperial, California 92251

Idaho State University
Vocational Technical School
Pocatello, Idaho 83209

Indiana Vocational Technical
College at Gary
Environmental Training
Coordination Center
1440 East 35th Avenue
Gary, Indiana 46409

J. Sargeant Reynolds Community
College
Ground Water Resources Program
P.O. Box 12084
Richmond, Virginia 23241

Jefferson State Junior College
Division of Social Sciences
Urban Planning and Development
Program
2601 Carson Road
Birmingham, Alabama 35215

Kansas Technical Institute
Civil Engineering Technology
    Department
2409 Scanlan Avenue
Salina, Kansas 67401

Kirkwood Community College
Environmental Studies and
    Pollution Control Department
Linn Hall
Cedar Rapids, Iowa 52406

Kilgore College
Occupational Education
Oil and Gas Technology
1100 Broadway
Kilgore, Texas 75662

Lane Community College
Department of Science
4000 East 30th Avenue
Eugene, Oregon 97405

Lees Junior College
Division of Science and
    Mathematics
Jackson, Kentucky 41339

Lee College
Occupational Education and
    Technology
Petroleum and Chemical Process
    Technology
P.O. Box 818
Baytown, Texas 77520

Lincoln Trails Community College
Vocational-Technical Education
    Programs
Route 3
Robinson, Illinois 62454

Linn-Benton Community College
Science & Technology Division
6500 S.W. Pacific Blvd.
Albany, Oregon 97321

Los Angeles Trade and Technical
    College
Science and Mathematics
    Department
400 West Washington Boulevard
Los Angeles, California 90015

Louisiana State University
Department of Engineering and
    Industrial Technology
Nuclear Science Center
Baton Rouge, Louisiana 70803

Louisiana Tech University
Department of Petroleum
    Engineering
P.O. Box 4875 Tech Station
Ruston, Louisiana 71272

Macomb County Community
    College
Occupational Program
14500 Twelve Mile Road
South Campus
Warren, Michigan 48089

Madisonville Community College
Coal Mining Technology Program
Madisonville, Kentucky 42431

Mankato State University
Biological Sciences Department
Mankato, Minnesota 56001

Medical College of Georgia
School of Allied Health Sciences
1120 15th Street
Augusta, Georgia 30901

Memphis State University
Center for Nuclear Studies
Memphis, Tennessee 38152

Miami-Dade Community College
Engineering Department
11011 S.W. 104th Street
Miami, Florida 33176

Midland College
Petroleum Technology Department
3600 North Garfield
Midland, Texas 79701

Milwaukee Area Technical College
Service and Health Occupations
 Division
1015 North Sixth Street
Milwaukee, Wisconsin 53203

Modesto Junior College
Engineering, Mathematics and
 Physical Sciences Department
College Avenue
Modesto, California 95350

Morehead State University
Applied Science and
 Technology Department
Morehead, Kentucky 40351

Mountain Empire Community
 College
Division of Technologies
Mining Technology Program
Big Stone Gap, Virginia 24219

Muskingum Area Technical College
Division of Engineering and Science
1555 Newark Road
Zanesville, Ohio 43701

New Mexico State University
Dona Ana County Occupational
 Education Branch
Las Cruces, New Mexico 88001

Niagara County Community
 College
Division of Technology,
 Mathematics and Physical
 Science
Environmental Studies Program
3111 Saunders Settlement Road
Sanborn, New York 14132

North Carolina State University
Interdepartmental Program in the
 School of Agriculture and Life
 Sciences
Raleigh, North Carolina 27611

North Dakota State School of
 Science
Technical Division
Environmental Science Technology
 Program
Wahpeton, North Dakota 58075

North Florida Junior College
Wastewater Treatment Department
Madison, Florida 32340

North Seattle Community College
Liberal Studies Department
9600 College Way North
Seattle, Washington 98103

North Shore Community College
Essex Agricultural and Technical
 Institute
3 Essex Street
Beverly, Massachusetts 01915

Northeastern Oklahoma A & M
 College
Agricultural Science and Industry
 Division
Second and I Streets, N.E.
Miami, Oklahoma 74354

Northern Montana College
Environmental Health Technology
 Department
Havre, Montana 59501

Northern Virginia Community
 College
Environmental and Natural
 Sciences Division
Woodbridge Campus
15200 Smoketown Road
Woodbridge, Virginia 22191

Northwestern Connecticut
  Community College
Environmental Technology
  Program
Park Place
Winsted, Connecticut 06098

Oak Ridge Associated Universities
Medical and Health Sciences
  Division
P.O. Box 117
Oak Ridge, Tennessee 37830

Orange Coast College
Division of Consumer and Health
  Science
2701 Fairview Road
Costa Mesa, California 92626

Oregon Institute of Technology
Division of Allied Health
  Technologies
Oretech Post Office
Klamath Falls, Oregon 97601

Oscar Rose Junior College
Environmental Science Department
6420 S.E. 15th Street
Midwest City, Oklahoma 73110

Palomar College
Vocational Education Department
1140 West Mission Road
San Marcos, California 92069

Pennsylvania State University
Air Pollution and Control
  Engineering Technology
  Department
University Park, Pennsylvania
  16802

Pennsylvania State University
Department of Nuclear Engineering
231 Sackett Building
University Park, Pennsylvania
  16802

Pennsylvania State University
Department of Petroleum and

Natural Gas Engineering
  (Mining)
118 Mineral Sciences Building
University Park, Pennsylvania
  16802

Pensacola Junior College
Water and Wastewater Operators
  Training Program
Route 8, Box 670 G
Pensacola, Florida 32505

Phoenix College
Technology Department
1202 West Thomas
Phoenix, Arizona 85013

Pikeville College
Department of Mining Technology
Pikeville, Kentucky 41501

Pikes Peak Community College
Division of Science and Math
5675 South Academy Boulevard
Colorado Springs, Colorado 80906

Pitt Technical Institute
Agricultural Programs
P.O. Drawer 7007
Greenville, North Carolina 27834

Polk Community College
Water and Wastewater Treatment
  Program
999 Avenue H, N.E.
Winter Haven, Florida 33880

Prince George's Community
  College
Urban and Environmental Studies
  Program
301 Largo Road
Largo, Maryland 20870

Queens College
Nuclear Medical Technology
  Department
1900 Sewlyn Avenue
Charlotte, North Carolina 28274

Rhode Island Junior College
Division of Vocational Technology
　Education
Knight Campus
Warwick, Rhode Island 02886

Roane State Community College
Division of Career Education
　(Nuclear Engineering Technology)
Harriman, Tennessee 37748

Roger Williams College
Division of Engineering
Bristol, Rhode Island 02809

Robeson Technical Institute
Pesticides and Fertilizers Program
Drawer A
Lumberton, North Carolina 28358

St. Cloud Area Vocational
　Technical Institute
Water and Waste Treatment
　Technology
1540 Northway Drive
St. Cloud, Minnesota 56301

Salem Community College
Chemistry Department
P.O. Box 551
Penn Grove, New Jersey 08069

Santa Ana College
Water Utility Science Department
17th at Bristol
Santa Ana, California 92706

Shoreline Community College
Division of Science and Social
　Science
16101 Greenwood Avenue, North
Seattle, Washington 98133

Southern Maine Vocational and
　Technical Institute
Wastewater Treatment Technology
　Department
2 Fort Road
South Portland, Maine 04106

Southern Technical Institute
Electrical Engineering Technology
　Department
(Nuclear Safety Option)
534 Clay Street
Marietta, Georgia 30060

Southern West Virginia Community
　College
Mining Education
Williamson, West Virginia 25661

State Fair Community College
Vocational/Technical Education
　Department
1900 Clarendon Road
Sedalia, Missouri 65301

State Technical Institute at
　Memphis
Environmental Engineering
　Technology Department
5983 Macon Cove,
Memphis, Tennessee 38134

State University of New York at
　Alfred
Agricultural & Technical College
Alfred, New York 14802

State University of New York at
　Farmingdale
Biological Technology Program
Melville Road
Farmingdale, New York 11735

Southeast Community College
Division of Natural Sciences and
　Related Technologies
Cumberland, Kentucky 40823

Southwest Virginia Community
　College
Division of Engineering
Mining Technology
P.O. Box SVCC
Richlands, Virginia 24641

Sullivan County Community
  College
Civil Technology Department
Loch Sheldrake, New York 12759

Sumter Area Techncial College
Technical Division (Agricultural
  Chemicals and Mechanization
  Technology)
506 Guignard Drive
Sumter, South Carolina 29150

Texas State Technical Institute
Nuclear Technology Program
Waco, Texas 76705

Tri County Technical College
Nuclear Engineering Technology
  Department
P.O. Box 87
Pendleton, South Carolina 29670

Trident Technical College
Chemical and Nuclear Engineering
Central Office
5290 Rivers Avenue
North Charleston, South Carolina
  29406

Trinidad State Junior College
Mining Technology Department
Trinidad, Colorado 81082

Tulsa Junior College
Scientific and Medical Services
  Division
Tenth and Boston
Tulsa, Oklahoma 74119

Tyler Junior College
Petroleum Technology Department
Tyler, Texas 75701

Ulster County Community College
Science Laboratory Technology
  Department
Stone Ridge, New York 12142

The University of the District of
  Columbia
Environmental Science Department
4200 Connecticut Avenue, N.W.
Washington, D.C. 20008

University of Lowell
Wastewater Treatment Department
Civil Engineering Technology
Lowell, Massachusetts 01854

University of Nevada at Las Vegas
College of Allied Health
  Professions
4505 Maryland Parkway
Las Vegas, Nevada 89154

University of New Hampshire
College of Life Sciences and
  Agriculture
Durham, New Hampshire 03824

University of Puerto Rico
Environmental Technology
  Program
Aquadella Campus
Aquadella, Puerto Rico 00603

Vermilion Community College
Technical Program
1900 East Camp Street
Ely, Minnesota 55731

Ventura College
Water Science Department
4667 Telegraph Road
Ventura, California 93003

Wake Technical Institute
Nuclear Engineering Technology
  Program
Route 10, Box 200
Raleigh, North Carolina 27603

Westchester Community College
Mathematics and Science Program
75 Grasslands Road
Valhalla, New York 10595

West Georgia College
Interdisciplinary Program in
  Environmental Studies
Carrollton, Georgia 30118

West Virginia Institute of
  Technology
Mining Engineering Technology
  Program
Montgomery, West Virginia 25136

West Virginia Northern Community
  College
Department of Occupational Safety
  and Environmental Hygiene
No. 1 College Square
Wheeling, West Virginia 26003

Western Nevada Community
  College
Arts and Sciences Department
Environmental Studies Program
2201 West Nye Lane
Carson City, Nevada 89701

Western Piedmont Community
  College
Natural Science and Mathematics
  Department
Morgantown, North Carolina 28655

Wilkes Community College
Food and Environmental Science
  Technologies Department
Collegiate Drive
Wilkesboro, North Carolina 28697

Chapter IX

Legal, Social, and Health Science Careers That Aid the Environment

In the 1960's our society realized that we are dependent on and part of an ecosystem that we did not invent and must not destroy. Public concern for environmental controls became intense. National, state, and local governments enacted laws to protect the land, the water, the air, and the workplace. New occupations have developed that consider the needs of the citizens, the entrepreneurs, and the planet. This chapter discusses several social science and health areas where people specialize in environmental protection.

A. THE LEGAL ASPECTS OF ENVIRONMENTAL PROTECTION

1. *The Environmental Protection Agency*

In 1970 the Environmental Protection Agency (EPA) was created by Congress to provide a broad, comprehensive approach to the solution of environmental problems. A number of important laws have given great strength and wide jurisdiction to this agency.

According to the *Clean Air Act*, the EPA is required to protect the public health and general welfare by establishing national air quality standards for all important air pollutants. Standards have already been set for particulate matter, sulfur oxides, hydrocarbons, carbon monoxide, photochemical oxidants, and nitrogen oxides. In addition, the EPA is required to set limits on the level of air pollutants emitted from such stationary sources as new power plants, municipal incinerators, factories, and chemical plants. The agency is also required to establish emission standards for new motor vehicles, as well as for hazardous air pollutants such as beryllium, mercury, asbestos, and vinyl chloride.

The *Clean Water Act* prohibits discharge of any pollutant into navigable water without a permit. The EPA, or states authorized by the EPA, may issue such permits based on the toxicity of the pollutant and, for nontoxic pollutants, based on the best pollution control technology available. The dumping of radioactive waste into the nation's waters is prohibited. The EPA is authorized to issue construction grants to aid municipalities in building wastewater treatment plants and to assist states in areawide waste treatment management planning. The EPA is required to conduct extensive research on all aspects of water pollution. The *Safe Water Act* makes the EPA responsible for setting minimum national drinking-water regulations.

The *Toxic Substances Control Act* authorizes the EPA to regulate the production and use of chemicals harmful to public health or the environment. The agency is required to compile a list of all such chemicals (now over 35,000) on the market, to limit the use of those found to be harmful, and, if necessary, to ban their production. A special section of the law bans the manufacture of PCB's (polychlorinated biphenyls). Formerly used in paints, inks, plastics, and as insulating fluids in electrical equipment, PCB's are poisonous to humans; they accumulate in the fatty tissue of fish and resist natural decay in the environment.

The EPA is also responsible for carrying out the provisions of the *Resource Conservation and Recovery Act*, which covers hazardous wastes, the *Federal Insecticide, Fungicide, and Rodenticide Act*, the *Noise Control Act*, the *Ocean Dumping Act*, and several others.

In January 1970 the President signed into law the National Environmental Policy Act (NEPA), which declared a national directive to encourage productive and enjoyable harmony between man and the environment. The NEPA requires each Federal agency to prepare a statement of environmental impact in advance of any major action that may significantly affect the quality of the environment. Such actions may include new highway construction, harbor dredging or filling, nuclear power plant construction, large-scale aerial pesticide spraying, river channeling, munitions disposal, and bridge construction.

Each statement must assess in detail the potential environmental impact of a proposed action, and all Federal agencies are required to prepare statements for matters under their jurisdiction. Each environmental impact statement must include:

- A detailed description of the proposed action including information and technical data adequate to permit a careful assessment of environmental impact;
- Discussion of the probable impact on the environment, including any impact on ecological systems and any direct or indirect consequences that may result from the action;

- Adverse environmental effects that cannot be avoided;
- Alternatives to the proposed action that might avoid some or all of the adverse environmental effects, including analysis of costs and environmental impacts of alternatives;
- An assessment of the cumulative, long-term effects of the proposed action including its relationship to short-term use of the environment versus the environment's long-term productivity;
- Any irreversible or irretrievable commitment of resources that might result from the action or that would curtail beneficial use of the environment.

2. Citizen Groups

Many fields and occupations are involved in the legalities of environmental protection. Usually three sides are represented in environmental suits today: the government, industry, and citizen action committees. All must be well prepared in their arguments for and against new developments.

The public participation of citizen organizations is an essential force for environmental improvement. Citizen organizations can focus public attention on what is and is not being done. They articulate the public's concern and attract press attention, which, in turn, helps nurture the climate of public opinion necessary for action. Citizen groups have the dedication, drive, and independence to carry on three fundamental missions in pursuit of a better environment:

- To insure adequate protection laws at the community, state, and Federal levels, and adequate appropriations and staff to carry out those laws;
- To encourage control agencies and polluters to move steadily toward compliance with environmental laws;
- To keep the public informed of the success or failure of environmental programs.

A few of the voluntary citizen groups that are dedicated to environmental protection are listed below. Many have state or local chapters or affiliates. The Commission for the Advancement of Public Interest Organizations (1875 Connecticut Avenue NW, Washington, DC 20009) publishes a series of guides listing all regional and national groups.

Environmental Conservation

Environmental Action, 1346 Connecticut Avenue, Washington, DC 20036

Environmental Defense Fund, 444 Park Avenue South, New York, NY 10016

Environmental Policy Center, 317 Pennsylvania Avenue SE, Washington, DC 20003

Friends of the Earth, 124 Spear Street, San Francisco, CA 94111

Natural Resources Defense Council, 122 East 42nd Street, New York, NY 10168

National Audubon Society, 950 Third Avenue, New York, NY 10022

National Wildlife Federation, 1412 16th Street NW, Washington, DC 20036

Sierra Club, 530 Bush Street, San Francisco, CA 94108

Wilderness Society, 1901 Pennsylvania Avenue NW, Washington, DC 20006

Energy

Alternative Sources of Energy, Milaca, MN 56353

Citizen/Labor Energy Coalition, 1300 Connecticut Avenue NW, Washington, DC 20036

Consumer Energy Council, 2000 L Street NW, Washington, DC 20036

Energy Action, 2000 P Street NW, Washington, DC 20036

The Solar Lobby, 1001 Connecticut Avenue NW, Washington, DC 20036

Urban Redevelopment

National Association of Neighborhoods, 1651 Fuller Street NW, Washington, DC 20009

The Urban Institute, 2100 M Street NW, Washington, DC 20037

National Council for Urban Economic Development, 1730 K Street NW, Washington, DC 20036

National Association of Housing & Redevelopment Officials, 2600 Virginia Avenue, Washington, DC 20006

Urban Environmental Conferences, 666 11th Street NW, Washington, DC 20005

Human Environmental Center, 1302 18th Street NW, Washington, DC 20036

Agriculture

National Farmers Union, 1012 14th Street NW, Washington, DC 20005

National Farmers Organization, 475 L'Enfant Plaza SW, Washington, DC 20514

National Grange, 1616 H Street NW, Washington, DC 20036

Organized Labor

AFL-CIO, 815 16th Street NW, Washington, DC 20006

United Auto Workers, 1757 N Street NW, Washington, DC 20036

National Education Association, 1201 16th Street, Washington, DC 20036

Association for Union Democracy, 215 Park Avenue South, New York, NY 10003

Political Action

Americans for Democratic Action, 1411 K Street NW, Washington, DC 20006

Common Cause, 2030 M Street NW, Washington, DC 20036

Democratic Agenda, 1346 Connecticut Avenue NW, Washington, DC 20036

Antinuclear Groups

Nuclear Information and Resource Service, 1536 16th Street NW, Washington, DC 20005

Mobilization for Survival, 3601 Locust Walk, Philadelphia, PA 19104

Union of Concerned Scientists, 1025 15th Street NW, Washington, DC 20005

Task Force Against Nuclear Pollution, 153 E Street SE, Washington, DC 20003

Physicians for Social Responsibility, Box 295, Cambridge, MA 02238

Council for a Liveable World, 100 Maryland Avenue NE, Washington, DC 20002

3. *Environmental Lawyer*

Environmental lawyers advise clients on environmental control laws and regulations. They may deal with many environmental issues or specialize, such as in wildlife conservation, noise control, or air resource management.

The environmental lawyer interprets laws and court decisions, which are often unclear and confusing, and applies them to varied situations.

Much of a lawyer's time is spent in library work, reading and summarizing cases to determine precedents. The lawyer also helps to write new laws, trying to word them so that they will be clear and easy to enforce.

Taking a case to court is slow and expensive. When possible, agreement is reached out of court. An environmental lawyer negotiates with violators as to how soon and by what means violations will be corrected.

After graduation from high school, it takes seven years of study to become a lawyer. For environmental law, while attending four years of college and law school, it would be helpful also to take science courses, if possible. Admission to law school is competitive, and a good scholastic record is necessary. Environmental lawyers need a year of experience in environmental law and must pass a bar examination.

Environmental lawyers work in government agencies, citizens' organizations, large industrial firms, and in private practice.

Environmental lawyers are being hired, but the openings are competitive. There may be more opportunities as the public becomes increasingly aware of the need for a healthful environment.

4. *Environmental Lobbyist*

Environmental lobbyists promote legislation to save natural resources. It is their job to make the environmentalist viewpoint heard above the voices of many others trying to influence legislators. Their concerns include air and water quality, noise abatement, and wildlife protection.

Environmental lobbyists testify at congressional, state legislative, and municipal hearings. They meet with politicians, instruct volunteers in persuasive techniques, and attend meetings of government agencies. They meet with reporters and newscasters to encourage news coverage of their viewpoints. They visit organizations and organize cooperative action to save our resources.

About half the environment lobbyist's time is spent in persuasion and half in research to keep up to the minute on laws and regulations. The lobbyist must be able to back his or her ideals with strong economic and environmental details.

Most environmental lobbyists have college coursework in journalism, public relations, mass media communications, or political science. Some have advanced degrees in law or science. Experience in speaking, writing, organizing, lobbying, or campaigning can be acquired as a volunteer worker.

Most environmental lobbyists work in Washington, D.C., but some are assigned to state capitals or large metropolitan areas. They may specialize in one problem or promote many environmental issues in which their organizations are interested.

Organizations having lobbyists include some of the environmental groups, such as the Sierra Club, other associations of concerned citizens, unions, and political groups. The *Conservation Directory* (Washington: National Wildlife Federation, 1412 16th Street, NW, Washington, DC 20036) lists many national organizations involved in protecting the environment.

On the other side of the issue, major corporations have lobbyists on their staffs who negotiate with politicians to present the feasibility of industrial growth within the safeguards of conservation. Often both sides can work together to provide regulations that protect the planet and its species, but allow economic development.

5. *Environmental Economist*

Environmental economists conduct research, prepare reports, and formulate plans to aid in solving economic problems arising from the production and distribution of goods and the negative environmental conditions that are generated as a result of new technologies. They prepare research studies and reports on the possible impact of environmental standards on industry. They predict overall costs and benefits of environmental programs. They help in finding least costly control methods.

Environmental economists work to provide a better understanding of economic principles and how they relate to environmental problems. They show how theories and principles of economic growth, cost-benefit analysis, and the market-pricing mechanism can aid us in protecting our natural resources and improving the quality of life.

It is difficult to put a price tag on environmental quality. However, many of these specialists believe that economic pressures are a key to the proper use and development of our resources.

Usually a bachelor's degree with a major in economics is the minimum educational requirement. It is more probable that a graduate degree will be required by an employer.

There are now as many economists in the United States as dentists. There are approximately 115,000 working economists. Roughly 10 percent of these economists work for the government, another 10 percent teach, and most of the rest are employed in private industry. Increased job opportunities are expected for economists who specialize in environmental problems. They work as members of environmental teams involved in planning development for communities, states, and the Federal government. Some act as consultants to industry, business, and private environmental groups.

B. THE HEALTH ASPECTS OF ENVIRONMENTAL PROTECTION

1. The Occupational Safety and Health Administration

In 1970 the Congress considered the yearly toll on the more than ninety million working Americans:

Job-related accidents accounted for more than 14,000 worker deaths.
Nearly 2½ million workers were disabled.
Ten times as many person-days were lost from job-related disabilities as from strikes.
300,000 new cases of occupational diseases were estimated.

In terms of lost production and wages, medical expenses, and disability compensation, the burden on the nation's commerce was staggering. Human cost was beyond calculation. Therefore, the Occupational Safety and Health Act was passed by a bipartisan Congress "... to assure so far as possible every working man and woman in the nation safe and healthful working conditions and to preserve our human resources." Under the Act, the Occupational Safety and Health Administration (OSHA) was created within the Department of Labor to:

- Encourage employers and employees to reduce workplace hazards and to implement new or improved existing safety and health programs;
- Provide for research in occupational safety and health and develop innovative ways of dealing with occupational safety and health problems;
- Establish "separate but dependent responsibilities and rights" for employers and employees for the achievement of better safety and health conditions;
- Maintain a reporting and recordkeeping system to monitor job-related injuries and illnesses;
- Establish training programs to increase the number and competence of occupational safety and health personnel;
- Develop mandatory job safety and health standards and enforce them effectively; and
- Provide for the development, analysis, evaluation, and approval of state occupational safety and health programs.

If you have any questions or are interested in seeking employment with OSHA, contact the office in your region:

Region I (CT, ME, MA, NH, RI, VT)
16-18 North Street
Boston, MA 02109

Region II (NY, NJ, PR, VI)
1515 Broadway
New York, NY 10036

Region III (DE, DC, MD, PA, VA, WV)
3535 Market Street
Philadelphia, PA 19104

Region IV (AL, FL, GA, KY, MS, NC, SC, TN)
1375 Peachtree Street, NE
Atlanta, GA 30367

Region V (IL, IN, MI, MN, OH, WI)
230 South Dearborn Street
Chicago, IL 60604

Region VI (AR, LA, NM, OK, TX)
555 Griffin Square
Dallas, TX 75202

Region VII (IA, KS, MO, NE)
911 Walnut Street
Kansas City, MO 64106

Region VIII (CO, MT, ND, SD, UT, WY)
1961 Stout Street
Denver, CO 80294

*Region IX (CA, AZ, NV, HI, Guam, American Samoa, Trust Territory
of the Pacific Islands)*
450 Golden Gate Avenue
Box 36017
San Francisco, CA 94102

Region X (AK, ID, OR, WA)
909 First Avenue
Seattle, WA 98174

2. Health and Regulatory Inspectors

Protecting the public from health and safety hazards, prohibiting
unfair trade and employment practices, preventing entry of prohibited
matter, and raising revenue are responsibilities of government. Health

and regulatory inspectors enforce the laws and regulations that govern those responsibilities.

a. *Health Inspectors*

Health inspectors work with engineers, chemists, microbiologists, and health workers to insure compliance with public health and safety regulations governing food, drugs, cosmetics, and other consumer products. They also administer regulations that govern the quarantining of persons and products entering the United States from foreign countries. The major types of health inspectors are: *consumer safety, food, agricultural quarantine*, and *environmental health inspectors*.

Most *consumer safety inspectors* specialize in food, feeds and pesticides, weights and measures, cosmetics, or drugs and medical equipment inspection. Working individually or in teams under a senior or supervisory inspector, they periodically check firms that produce, handle, store, and market food, drugs, and cosmetics. They look for inaccurate product labeling and for decomposition or chemical or bacteriological contamination that could result in a product's becoming harmful to health. They use portable scales, cameras, ultraviolet lights, contane sampling devices, thermometers, chemical testing kits, radiation monitors, and other equipment to detect violations. They send product samples collected as part of their examinations to laboratories for analysis.

After completing their inspection, inspectors discuss their observations with plant managers or officials and point out areas where corrective measures are needed. They write reports of their findings and, when necessary, compile evidence that may be used in court if legal action must be taken to enforce the law.

Federal and state laws empower *food inspectors* to inspect meat, poultry, and their by-products to insure that they are wholesome and safe for public consumption. Working as an on-site team under a veterinarian, they inspect meat and poultry slaughtering, processing, and packaging operations. They also check for correct product labeling and proper sanitation.

Agricultural quarantine inspectors protect American agricultural products from the spread of foreign plant pests and animal diseases. To safeguard crops, forests, gardens, and livestock, they inspect ships, aircraft, railroad cars, and motor vehicles entering the United States for restricted or prohibited plant or animal materials.

Environmental health inspectors work primarily for state and local governments or for the EPA. They insure that food, water, and air meet government standards. They check the cleanliness and safety of food and beverages produced in dairies and processing plants or served in restaurants, hospitals, and other institutions. They often examine the handling, processing, and serving of food for compliance with sanitary rules and regulations. They oversee the treatment and disposal of sewage, refuse, and garbage. They examine places where pollution is a danger, test for pollutants, and collect air or water samples for analysis. They determine the nature and cause of pollution and initiate action to stop it.

In large local and state health or agricultural departments, environmental health inspectors may specialize in milk and dairy products, food sanitation, waste control, air pollution, institutional sanitation, or occupational health. In rural areas and small cities, they may be responsible for a wide range of environmental health activities.

b. *Regulatory Inspectors*

Occupational safety and health inspectors visit places of employment to detect unsafe or unhealthful working conditions. They inspect machinery and equipment and observe en.ployees to see that safety equipment is used and precautions are taken in accordance with Federal, state, or local government standards and regulations.

Occupational safety and health inspectors usually visit a plant, factory, or other workplace in response to a complaint or an accident. In their reports, they describe hazards and cite safety standards or regulations that have been violated. They also discuss their findings with the employer or plant manager and urge that violations be promptly corrected.

c. *Employment and Training for Health and Regulatory Inspectors*

Health and regulatory inspectors held over 101,000 jobs in 1982. About 36 percent were employed by the Federal government, 34 percent by state governments, and the rest by local governments.

The largest single employer of consumer safety inspectors is the U.S. Food and Drug Administration, but the majority work for state governments. Most food inspectors are employed by the U.S. Department of Agriculture. Most environmental health inspectors work for state and local governments. Occupational safety and health inspectors work for the Department of Labor, as well as for many state governments.

Because of the wide range of inspector jobs and varying starting levels, qualifications for employment differ greatly. Requirements are a combination of education, experience, and a written examination. Generally, agencies prefer applicants who are college graduates and whose course work is related to the job. Food inspectors must have related experience and pass an examination based on specialized knowledge. Environmental health inspectors and occupational safety inspectors usually must have a bachelor's degree in the physical or biological sciences. Some community colleges offer programs for inspectors.

All inspectors are trained in applicable laws and inspection procedures through a combination of classroom and on-the-job training. In addition, people who want to become health and regulatory inspectors should like detailed work and be able to accept responsibility. They should be neat and personable and able to express themselves well orally and in writing.

Inspectors whose job performance is satisfactory advance through their career ladder to a specified full performance level. Above this level (usually supervisory positions), advancement is competitive, based on agency needs and individual merit.

d. *Job Outlook and Earnings for Health and Regulatory Inspectors*
Employment of health and regulatory inspectors as a group is expected to increase more slowly than the average for all occupations through the mid-1990's. Employment growth is expected to be constrained by slow growth in government regulatory programs and in government spending. Most job openings will be to replace those who transfer to other occupations, retire, or leave the labor force for other reasons. Most inspectors work in programs that enjoy wide public support. As a result, they are less likely to lose their jobs than many other workers when government programs are cut.

In the Federal government, the average starting salary for health and regulatory inspectors was $13,000 in 1982. Experienced inspectors had salaries ranging from $25,000 to $34,000. Starting health inspectors working for states averaged almost $17,000 in 1983.

3. *Occupational Health Physician and Occupational Health Nurse*

No one knows how many workers become ill because of job-related conditions. Unfortunately, many occupational diseases often go undetected for years.

Occupational physicians and nurses examine workers and diagnose and treat a variety of conditions. They give emergency treatment in accident cases and reexamine workers with disabilities to check on their progress. Many employers have their workers physically examined annually. The screening and testing programs, often administered by the nurse, include a variety of tests such as audiograms, (hearing tests), eye examinations, EKG examinations, blood tests, and X rays. These results are then reviewed by the physician, who decides what is needed.

Occupational health physicians have not had a strong record of detecting and controlling occupational diseases. In fact, most outbreaks of occupational diseases have been identified accidentally. Exposure to hazardous materials in a workplace often does not have an impact on the incidence of occupational illness for fifteen or twenty years. Today, a number of corporations are increasing their medical staffs.

In some plants, occupational health nurses conduct health and safety meetings and show workers how to protect their health. In some cases, they may visit work areas and report hazards, such as excessive noise or dust, to the management.

The occupational nurse and physician work as a team with industrial hygienists and industrial hygiene engineers to prevent accidents, illness, and disease.

Occupational health nurses are registered nurses, usually with some previous training and experience in emergency room techniques or industrial nursing. Certification by the American Board of Occupational Health Nurses (P.O. Box 638, Thousand Palms, CA 92276) requires a minimum of five years' recent full-time experience, 60 hours of specialized coursework, and a written examination.

The occupational health physician is a fully trained and licensed physician. At present, there are very few people who are especially trained in occupational medicine. Four years of college, with training in premedical courses, plus four years of medical school, plus one or two years of internship are the minimum requirement for licensing. Specialized training in diseases of the ear, occupational health, or public health may take many more years. Entry to this profession requires an excellent scholastic record.

Employers are placing increased emphasis on health services to employees and making the workplace safe. Because of increasing interest in preventive medicine, more stringent government requirements, and higher insurance rates, employment opportunities should be favorable for qualified occupational health nurses and physicians.

4. *Industrial Hygienist*

The industrial hygienist's work involves three interrelated functions: recognizing hazards and detecting their development promptly; evaluating their seriousness; and prescribing methods of eliminating or controlling them. Industrial hygienists may urge drastic changes in a process or even in an entire plant where unsafe conditions are found to exist. Where necessary, they may recommend costly modification or replacement of equipment. Frequently they order substitution of less toxic materials, even at the expense of greatly increased production costs. During emergencies they may even have authority to order a shutdown of operations when there is no time to confer with management.

Today, the industrial hygienist battles radiation, fungi, air pollution, noise, vibration, and poor lighting. The industrial hygienist is also concerned with protecting the worker against discomfort, fatigue, and other influences that may contribute to low morale and inefficiency.

Although most industrial hygienists work in industrial settings, many are employed by transportation companies and public utilities, state and local health departments, the Federal government, mining companies, large agricultural operations, insurance businesses, and commercial businesses. A few are self-employed as consultants.

Persons planning careers as industrial hygienists should be interested in science or engineering and have a strong desire to apply technical knowledge to practical situations. The basic educational requirement for industrial hygiene is a college degree with a major in engineering or one of the physical sciences. Certification is optional but desirable, and those possessing certification usually command higher salaries. Certification is obtained by passing an examination by the governing body, the American Board of Industrial Hygiene.

Continued expansion is anticipated in this profession over the next decade due to increased public interest in ecology and the concern for environmental health by all levels of government. Starting salaries for industrial hygienists with bachelor's degrees was approximately $18,000 in 1982, those with master's degrees $21,000, and those with doctorates approximately $26,000.

For information concerning a career in industrial hygiene write to:

American Industrial Hygiene Association
665 Miller Road
Akron, Ohio 44313

C. THE SOCIAL ASPECTS OF ENVIRONMENTAL PROTECTION

Social scientists study all aspects of human society, from the distribution of products and services to newly formed religious groups or plans for modern mass transportation systems. Social science research provides insights that help us understand the many ways in which persons and groups make decisions, exercise power, or respond to change. Through their studies and analyses, social scientists and urban planners assist educators, government officials, business leaders, and others to solve social, economic, and environmental problems. This section considers three occupations that deal directly with the relationship between everyday life and the environment.

1. Urban and Regional Planners

Urban and regional planners, often called community or city planners, develop programs to provide for future growth and revitalization of urban, suburban, and rural communities. They help local officials make decisions on social, economic, and environmental problems.

Planners examine community facilities such as health clinics and schools to be sure the facilities can meet the demands placed upon them. They keep abreast of the legal issues involved in community development or redevelopment and changes in housing and building codes. Urban and regional planners prepare for situations that are likely to develop as a result of population growth or social and economic change. They are responsible for predicting the environmental impact of new factories, housing, and public facilities. They must consider how sometimes a perceived improvement, such as a park, may jeopardize the ecological design.

A master's degree in planning, architecture, or engineering usually qualifies a person for an entry-level position. In 1982 about 80 colleges and universities offered a master's degree in urban or regional planning. Planners must be able to grasp spatial relationships and visualize the effects of their plans and designs. They should be flexible and able to reconcile different viewpoints to make constructive policy recommendations.

Employment of planners is expected to grow more slowly than the average for all occupations through the mid-1990's due to the slow growth in government spending. Some persons trained as planners may have to accept jobs in other areas of public policy and administration. Graduates of prestigious academic institutions should have the best job prospects. Urban and regional planning graduates who have specialized in economic development, land-use planning, transportation systems, or health systems may be in particular demand.

In 1981 urban and regional planners earned a median annual salary of about $26,000. Planners with a master's degree were hired by the Federal government at a starting salary of $19,700 in 1982. Salaries of planners employed by the Federal government averaged $34,000 in 1982.

Additional information is available from:

American Planning Association
1776 Massachusetts Avenue NW
Washington, DC 20036

2. *Land-Use Specialist*

Land planners find ways to solve human needs, such as those for open space, housing, clean air, and safe water, by planning ahead. It is less expensive to reserve open space for parks than to create parkland by razing buildings later. It is less expensive to locate an airport away from residential areas than to solve a noise problem after houses are built next to it.

The land planner may plan a small city park, a whole county, a transportation system, an urban renewal project, or a large recreational area.

First, the land planner meets with people who will be using the land and finds out their needs and preferences. The planner studies the land, its soil, water, wildlife, and other features, and checks to see what laws or regulations might limit use of the land and what plans have been made for surrounding areas. Computer and statistical analyses are used to consider the many variables involved. Finally the land planner proposes a system for locating various activities on the land and writes a report explaining the costs and benefits of the proposal.

Land planning is a relatively new field. Workers have come to planning from other fields with various combinations of education and experience, but the usual requirement is a master's degree in planning with training in related subjects, such as civil engineering, landscape architecture, public administration, natural science, or one of the social sciences. Land planners work for Federal, state, county, and regional agencies dealing with land management, conservation, health, transportation, building, zoning, parks, and municipal planning. Land planning is a growing field, and probably more planners will be needed.

3. *Landscape Architect*

Landscape architects plan and design developments of land areas for projects, such as parks and recreational facilities, airports, highways, and parkways. They also work on projects involving hospitals, schools, land subdivisions, commercial zones, industrial sites, and housing developments.

First, they carefully analyze the site. They compile and analyze data on site conditions, geographic features, and location of structures in order to prepare the environmental impact report and develop landscaping plans.

They prepare site plans, working drawings, specifications, and cost estimates for land development. These drawings show ground contours, vegetation, location of structures, and such facilities as roads, walks, parking areas, fences, walls, and utilities. They coordinate the arrangement of existing and proposed land features and structures. They also build three-dimensional models to show how their proposals will look.

Usually the landscape architect stays with the project until its completion, directing construction. Visits to the site may continue after completion, to be sure that the client can maintain the project.

The minimum educational requirement is a bachelor's degree in architecture with coursework in ecology, the behavioral and social sciences, regional and environmental planning, and art, science, math, and computer studies. In thirty-eight states a landscape architect is required to pass a licensing examination to practice independently.

About half of the landscape architects are employed by the government. Much of the work is related to the development of forest and park management. Others work for corporations and architectural and engineering firms, and many are self-employed.

Construction projects have been hard to finance within the last ten years, and few jobs are available for new landscape architects. Also, many builders do not see a need for this added design. Among land developers, however, prospects appear relatively good if interest rates come down.